LEAD AND MANAGE

The four cornerstones

by

Frank MacHovec PhD

Copyright © 2007 Frank MacHovec
ISBN 978-0-6151-6410-6
All rights reserved
Printed in the United States of America

Work is an extension of personality.
It is achievement. and one of the ways
people define themselves, measure
their worth and their humanity.
-- Peter Drucker (1977)

ACKNOWLEDGMENTS

Sources are cited in the text and listed in the references at the end of chapters in keeping with fair use copyright law.

ABOUT THIS BOOK

There are many books and manuals on leadership skills. Some focus only on leadership skills and others on management skills. This book blends both because good leaders can and should be good managers and good managers must also lead effectively. Unlike others, this book applies psychological concepts to enrich leadership skills.

Some books and manuals are mostly theoretical with little or no practical exercises to experience and apply theory to work realities. Still others lean toward the academic in almost encyclopedic detail difficult to understand. This book has distilled the leadership and management skills from thirty years of field-testing in workshops and training programs in the U.S. and Canada. The goal was to present theory briefly, with exercises to apply theory to practice.

The four cornerstones to lead or manage are basic skill areas. Each is described in a separate chapter. The first is self-awareness or intrapersonal awareness, knowing who you are, your strengths and weaknesses. The second is other-awareness or inter-personal awareness, understanding others, how they differ and are likely to interact with you. The third is coaching skills or group dynamics, how best to lead a team, department, or organization. The fourth is task management, getting the job done, and blends skills developed in the other three areas.

How does this book differ from all the others? It is more concise, simpler in focus and format on only four skill areas, with 94 exercises to experience the concept, practice it, and apply it immediately on the job. These advantages can be seen by side-by-side comparison with other manuals. Such a comparison is in itself a practical exercise to develop leadership skill!

ABOUT THE AUTHOR

Frank MacHovec has spent his career combining the academic-scientific with hands-on management experience to create and conduct communications and leadership skills training throughout the U. S. and Canada. This book is a distillation of 50 years of field-tested programs. His experience as an instructor in amphibious warfare in the Marine Corps during the Korean War. After his military service, he rose from office jobs to sales then management positions with Rand McNally, McGraw-Hill, and John Wiley publishers. He earned BA, MA, and PhD degrees during those years.

After a mid-career change, he spent 30 years in clinics, hospitals, and private practice as a licensed psychologist but continued to teach, write, create and conduct training programs, and speak at state, national, and international conferences. He has authored more than 30 books, many magazine and journal articles, and he has appeared on nationwide TV and radio. He was statewide Director of Quality Assurance for the Virginia Department of Mental Health, responsible for staff training in 11 hospitals and licensing hundreds of clinics and group homes. He was awarded a National Certificate of Recognition by Division 12 (Psychologists in Public Service) of the American Psychological Association. He is past president of the Virginia Association for Marriage and Family Therapy and was director of the leadership academy of the Coast Guard Auxiliary, 5th District which field-teted the material in this manual.

CONTENTS

SKILL 1: WHO ARE YOU?
Self-awareness

The four basic skills; you are unique; forces that shape you; obstacles to perception; needs, unmet and sick; self-actualization; personality, yours and theirs; building self-confidence; fight burnout.

SKILL 2: WHO ARE THESE OTHERS?
Interpersonal awareness

Listening skills; body language; verbal defenses; interacting and transacting; problem people; when you are the problem; talk tactics; mentoring; counseling skills.

SKILL 3: MOTIVATE AND MENTOR!
Coaching and team building

Your team experience; team or just group; group power; self-test; winning and losing teams; ideal team members; managerial grid; transformational leadership; facets of team leadership; leader tactics; dissatisfiers and satisfiers; time and timing; managing meetings; neutralize negatives; workplace violence; preventing suicide.

SKILL 4: GET IT DONE!
You as taskmaster

Envision and actualize; when to lead, follow, or delegate; decision making and problem solving; the scientific method; change; conflict management; coping skills; evaluating people and programs.

SKILL 1

WHO ARE YOU?
Self-awareness

Are leaders born or made? Historians still debate this question. Do the best leaders have a genetic gift, knowledge, skill, and ability, or do leaders emerge when there is a need for them? That question has puzzled historians wonder if it is a leader who shapes the times or do the needs of the time cause leaders to rise to power. Human behavior is complex and multi-causational. Current research suggests who we are and who we become result from interaction of both hereditary and environmental factors. So, leadership involves nature and nurture, the man or woman and the times.

Sometimes leadership "comes with the territory" as part of a job description, the result of promotion or by appointment. It can be serendipitous, a matter of luck, being the right person at the right time. History offers many examples of leadership used for good and for evil. Hitler and Stalin were leaders on the dark side of human nature and Moses, Buddha, Jesus, and Muhammad led people toward spiritual light.

Whether leaders are born or made, learning more about it and how to use it can hone leadership skills to a fine edge. That is the goal of this book. It can be used as a self-help guide individually or in a group as a shared training manual. Each of the four chapters focuses on one of the four basic skills: self-awareness (who are you?), other-awareness (who are these other people?), team building (you as coach), and task management (getting things done). There are 94 exercises throughout the book to help you learn, experience, and immediately apply what is learned.

Effective leaders learn to manage themselves before they attempt to lead others. For that reason self-awareness, getting to know yourself, is the first leadership skill to develop. It is the solid foundation for the other leadership skills. Socrates' admonished his students "know thyself," advice as true today as when he voiced it in ancient Greece. It means feeling comfortable with who and what you are, aware of strengths and weaknesses, minimizing one and maximizing or at least optimizing the other. The leadership skills in this book are based on three questions as basic to mental health as they are to effective leadership.

    1. Who am I?
    2. Who are these other people?
    3. What the hell am I doing?

The four skill areas in this manual will help you to answer those questions. The first focuses on helping you better understand who *you* are, the second helps you understand *others* (interpersonal or other awareness), the third will help you improve team building skills, and the fourth, how to get things done (task management). They will not only help you enrich your leaders-manager skills but also your personal and professional growth.

Effective leaders are sometimes described as people "who really know themselves" or "comfortable being themselves." These comments refer to leaders with high level of awareness of who they are. Socrates' admonition "know thyself" was also inscribed over ancient temple entrances with this added requirement: "Only the pure in heart may enter here." The Greeks valued self-awareness and their view of a pure heart meant being free of bias. In ancient times the heart also symbolized deep feelings, so a pure heart was not only free of bias but also of ill feelings. Today, we'd call that being objective, and the Greeks knew about it 2500 years ago.

This chapter's goal is to help you meet yourself and to be "pure in heart." Achieving that goal is like taking a mental shower to "clean up your act." You have to be able to see inside yourself before you can see inside others. It means you have to have the courage to see what's *really* there, not what you want to see or would like to see. When you do that you will be able to become a more real you and as a leader help others do the same. This does not mean being better at manipulating anyone (you included!) but to find meaning in your work and help others do so.

Why spend time and effort to understand yourself when there's work to be done? Leaders who are that impatient are like charging bulls. They're fast and full of energy but short on brains. Socrates chose his words carefully and what he said showed he knew a secret of effective leadership. That secret is you can't be self-confident, decisive, and effective as a leader unless and until you are aware of who you are and aren't. It is as important to know who you are as knowing what you're doing.

If self-awareness is weak, awareness of others will also be weak. This includes a realistic view of strengths and weaknesses and the skill of using strengths and controlling for weaknesses. It takes time and effort to recognize, understand, and process the factors and forces that shaped you into who you are. You will then be able to put it all in perspective and become the *best you*, do your best as a leader or manager, understand and adapt to others, and build a team that can achieve goals well. Try this skill builder exercise to help you see into yourself:

SKILL BUILDER 1. A classic question from Europe's existentialist philosophers was: "You are free, define yourself!" Without using your name, age, gender, politics, religion, race, or national origin, describe who you are in as many ways you can. It may not be easy!

Artists, poets, composers, and philosophers have spent their lives reflecting on this aspect of their identity. It helps them express themselves in their work more freely and effectively. Michelangelo and DaVinci in art, Shakespeare in literature, Tchaikovsky and Beethoven in music, all did so and their works show it. Even those who were troubled like Van Gogh and Lautrec showed a "search for self" in what they produced. In science, the arts and humanities, self-awareness and self-expression have been major themes worldwide throughout history, evidence of their value and importance.

YOU ARE UNIQUE

You are truly one of a kind. Your fingerprint and DNA differ from everyone else. You differ in gender from half the people in the world. There are other differences, such as hair, eye, and skin color, height and weight. So, your personality differs from others because no one else has experienced exactly what you have, from birth to this moment. Most physical features are *hereditary*, gifts of nature and most psychological traits and behaviors are *environmental*, shaped by life experience, learning and and conditioning.

SKILL BUILDER 2. Make a list of your favorites:
- *(a) food*
- *(b) dessert*
- *(c) drink*
- *(d) car*
- *(e) sport*
- *(f) music*
- *(g) movie*
- *(h) actor and actress*
- *(i) leisure activity*
- *(j) color*

If you asked others to do this exercise would you expect the answers to be the same as yours? Unlikely. So, this exercise proves there are individual differences and that everyone is a unique individual.

FORCES THAT SHAPE YOU

From the day you were born many factors and forces shaped your personality and behavior. Because of what we have experienced we have unique viewpoints of the world, life, and people. What follows is a list of forces and factors you can explore to help you see what influenced your personality development and behavior. Reflect on each of them and how they may have influenced you. Being aware of them will help you avoid personal bias as you interact with others.

GENETIC TRAITS AND PREDISPOSITIONS

Genetic traits and *predispositions* are inherited from genes at the instant of conception. They determine race, native intelligence, fine motor skills, overall body build, and predispositions to certain medical or mental conditions. They are hereditary, therefore permanent, but the environment can have an effect on them. As children grow and develop they are taller or shorter, heavier or thinner, stronger or weaker than others their age. Salesmen tend to be taller than their peers. Napoleon was short and some historians suggest this contributed to his being more competitive and more daring in strategy. So, genetic "gifts of nature" can influence your self-concept and how well or poorly you are accepted by others.

Gender differences are genetic factors that can influence life and work. Men can't have babies. That's a genetic fact. Boys play games to compete and win. Girls play games more to have fun and share in it. That's both genetic and environmental (learned). Anthropologists say there is an evolutionary aspect to this. Males, from animal to human, have been hunters and females gatherers and nurturers. Of course, there are exceptions in strong women and weaker men. Here again, environment can make a difference. Parents, home, family, and opportunity are important factors. Boys and girls are raised differently. Equality in the work place and equal pay for equal work are accepted values though still not implemented everywhere.

We now know there are basic personality differences between men and women. Many researchers have studied this subject intensively and agree men tend to be loners and are more independent and competitive. Competing and winning are important to them. They focus on goals and think concretely through problems. Women are more social-relational, collaborative, more open emotionally.

The Rodin statue of the thinker, seated lost in thought, is a classic male figure. Other examples are art and statuary of David, Apollo, Moses, Buddha, and Jesus. These men stand alone as if asserting their individuality. Women are portrayed as more caring and giving or in a supportive relationship. Examples are Madonna with child, Isis with son Horus, and Artemis and Mary with arms reaching out. Psychologist Sandra Bem recommends more open sharing of masculine and feminine traits by both genders. She called this exchange of gifts *androgyny*. It doesn't mean that men become effeminate or women more masculine. Both genders would benefit. Women would be more comfortable being assertive and men more open to sharing their feelings.

Men and women who lead others should be aware of gender differences, the effect of learning and conditioning, and Bem's ideal of sharing strengths in a mutual relationship. The goal should be to blend positive traits without losing the qualities of uniqueness that both genders find attractive and valuable. It applies also to sharing with the disabled, minorities, and even eccentrics. Howard Hughes did not meet the criteria for "normal" but he was a creative genius. Without his ideas and innovations the defense and airline industries would not be where they are today.

SKILL BUILDER 3. Reflect on your gender. How well do you understand the opposite gender? How well do you understand your own gender? How can you learn more and further develop awareness and understanding? It will increase your unique strengths and enrich your leadership skill. It will also help you increase gender appreciation in those you lead.

ETHNICITY

Ethnicity is a word that is becoming applied to race, national origin, culture, and religion. Ethnic differences separate minorities from mainstream culture and bond minority members closer together. There are strengths and weaknesses on both sides. Freud wrote that being Jewish in Vienna as Nazis rose to power forced him to rely on himself more and develop independent judgment. If you are in a minority it can also distance you from others. Young people often move from "the old ways" when they meet and share with others outside their ethnic group. The Broadway hit show and movie *Fiddler on the Roof* began with the song *Tradition* and ended with young people moving away as times changed. Ethnicity can influence self-concept, attitude, behavior, and interaction with others.

COMMUNITY AND GROUP IDENTITY

There can be differences in values and behavior in differing subcultures by region, state, city, and even neighborhoods. Examples: "city folks" and "country folks," sports fans in opposing teams, regional differences north and south, east and west, and national differences. The popular Broadway show and movie *West Side Story* is an example of clashing cultures that lead to tragedy, but also how "love conquers all" overcoming differences. So, community and group identity have the potential to influence behavior ad shape personality. The effect can be negative or positive. Effective leaders foster family and fellow feeling that neutralizes the negatives and builds on the positives. They share the view of Terence in ancient Rome 2200 years ago: "I am human and nothing human is alien to me." Differences can be fascinating and can enrich the work place.

HOME AND FAMILY

Parents are your first teachers and role models. So are brothers, sisters, relatives, friends, neighbors, and teachers.

Those we look up to help shape our idea of who we'd like to be. Your parents sent messages like that throughout your childhood. They didn't go to "parent school" and like most paents, probably did the best they ccould. Not perfect, some of the effect may be negative. Parenting can be overdone or underdone. Overdoing is being over-protective, too strict, or over-controlling. That can lead to overdependence, low self-concept, feelings of entitlement, or resistance to authority. Underdoing can lead to feelings of abandonment or alienation, depression, or low self-esteem. Other negative parent styles are absentee, indifferent, substance abusing, or mentally ill parents. Birth order, where you rank by age and number and gender of brothers and sisters, also exert an influence on personality development.

SKILL BUILDER 4. Has your ethnicity, community identity, or family life influenced your behavior? Satisfaction and pride in them is normal but there is a negative potential if it stifles healthy personality development. You can become defensive, self-centered, or feel inferior if you let it get you down. Can you be proud of your heritage and neutralize any negatives? Is there anything that might prevent you from developing and maintaining positive family and fellow feeling with others?

FRIENDS

Friendships are how we learn to share and get along with others. We confide in our friends and they help us develop our own distinctive personalities. Ralph Waldo Emerson said: "Show me your friends and I'll know your real self." Effective leaders provide their staff with the same kind of caring and support of a good friend. Were there kids your age and gender to play with during your childhood?

THE SCHOOL EXPERIENCE

Your educational experiences have had an influence on you. Looking back, were your school years positive or negative? Is your memory of them happy or were they a bothersome chore, a hoop to jump through? Your first day of school as a child marked a dramatic change in your life. It meant leaving home, family, and favorite toys. Then you had to share with kids you didn't know in a new and strange place, with a grownup who told you what to do. Later there was homework, sometimes uninteresting subjects, tests, grades, and report cards. Effective leaders are like teachers and the best leaders know an effective way to teach is by example.

SOCIAL STATUS

Social scientists classify status into lower, middle, and upper, with three subgroups in each from upper-upper to low-low. Would you be any different if you were an upper-upper class billionaire? Any different if you were from a low-low social status? Unemployed? Homeless? Would your attitude and behavior be any different toward a billionaire? A lower class person? There is a celebrity status, special consideration based on fame or position. Would you react to a celebrity differently than people at your socio-economic level? How do you interact with those at a lower status level? How status-free are you, really? The best leaders adapt to people of all levels.

OCCUPATION, THE WORK WORLD

Career and work history can influence behavior on and off the job. How has your job training and work experience affected your leadership role? Are you a product of "the school of hard knocks," promoted up the line from an entry-level position? Or are you a specialist or expert uniquely qualified for your position? If so, there may be distance between you and the office staff. If you work alone, there may be distance between you and other specialists in similar positions. The best leaders are aware of these factors and take steps to ensure optimal working relationships. Are you able to do so? Have you?

***SKILL BUILDER 5.** Review these four factors for any negative influences. If none are apparent, how do you think they could affect others in a leadership role? Are you aware enough to detect significant differences with the skill to overcome them?*

Leaders need to be sensitive to and aware of bias in any situation, in themselves and in others. For you to develop this skill it's important to see what's there, not what you want to see or would like to see. Otherwise, there can be a hidden agenda that interferes with team building and work efficiency. Therapist Bill O'Hanlon described this realization process:

> To *realize* you need *real eyes* to see *real lies*
> to be able to say: *"Real I is!"*
> (ungrammatical but true!)

OBSTACLES TO PERCEPTION

There can be obstacles to clear perception that often go unnoticed that can interfere with communications with others. Here's a sampling:

1. Oversimplification, overgeneralizing, stereotyping.

These are unjustified judgments. They are *universals* wrongfully applied to everyone in the group mentioned. Most of the time the words *always, every, ever, never, all, whenever* are used or implied. The reality is few things in life are so certain. Here are four examples:

    (a) *Blondes have more fun.*
    It may be every blonde you've known *has* had more fun but this does *not* justify the statement as it stands which means *all* blondes *everywhere* and *forever* have more fun.

    (b) *It always rains on vacation.*
    Even if it has rained on every vacation you've had, you can't correctly say it will *always* rain on vacations, and that includes yours and everyone else's.

    (c) *Speed kills.*
    Certainly, driving at high speed increases braking distance and less time to correct for error, but a burst of speed might prevent an accident. As it stands, the statement means speed *always* kills, no exceptions.

(d) *Leaders don't manage well and managers don't lead well.*
Same basic error. It implies no leader can ever manage well and no manager can ever lead well. The opposite is also not true: *Leaders manage well and managers lead well.* Not necessarily. Today, leaders have to have good management skills and managers have to lead well.

SKILL BUILDER 6. Reword those statements into more valid and acceptable versions. Think of similar obstacles to clear thinking in your daily life and work. Listen to conversations on the street, socially, and on TV. Avoid making the same mistakes.

2. **Half-truth, card stacking, slanting, spinning, preconceived notion.**
All these reflect unwarranted bias based on insufficient information to justify a valid statement. It's like the old saying: "Statistics don't lie but liars use statistics." For instance:

(a) *What goes up must come down.*
Not in outer space! Even that isn't entirely valid because an object in space may or may not be drawn into the gravitational field of a planet, asteroid, or star and never come down anywhere. This bias is based on earthbound phenomena of falling objects and only partly true.

(b) *Airliners crash, therefore flying is dangerous.*
There *are* airliner crashes but statistically, as has been pointed out many times, flying is safer than driving a car.

(c) *Muslims are terrorists.*
Only a small fraction of Muslims are terrorists. There have been terrorists in other religions. As the statement stands, it means *all* Muslims are terrorists, an exaggerated opinion without factual or validation.

(d) *You have the flu because that's how I felt when I had it.*
Maybe, maybe not. One case does not prove a rule. Similar symptoms can occur in other diseases. Even if you're a medical doctor, such a statement is still only one opinion.

SKILL BUILDER 7. Reword the statements into more valid versions. Think of similar examples. Be able to rely on objective information and refute biased statements. Learn the value of words such as may or can, occasionally or sometimes, often or rarely, etc.

SKILL BUILDER 8. Advertising, news, talk shows, and political campaigns are opportunities to detect obstacles to clear perception. Use them and overheard everyday conversations to sharpen your ability to separate fact from bias and distortion. When Ernest Hemingway was asked the most useful skill of a writer he replied: "A 100% reliable BS detector!"

3. **Superstition, myth, and "isms."**

These are long disproved or useless beliefs based on custom, tradition, or just plain ignorance. An example of a superstition you may unknowingly use is blessing someone who sneezes. Why bless a sneeze that has blasted thousands of germs into the air? In the Middle Ages it was believed the soul is blown out of the body through the nose in a sneeze and the devil can then capture it. Blessing the person kept the devil away. Offering a facial tissue to a sneezer would be more helpful. Other examples of superstitions you may have heard:

(a) Never trust anyone who can't look you in the eye.
Some trustworthy people are shy and avoid eye contact.

(b) If you get wet, cold, or have a chill and you'll catch a cold.
Germs, not weather or temperature, cause colds.

(c) If you have a fever, tie garlic around your neck.
That might keep more people than germs away. There is no medical evidence that doing this has any effect on elevated body temperature.

(d) Never walk under a ladder.
You could be struck by a dropped tool or bucket of paint. But it's an old superstition based on religion. A ladder propped against a wall created a triangle, the symbol of the Holy Trinity, so walking through it was considered blasphemy.

SKILL BUILDER 9. *Can you think of any superstitions you still have or have heard from others? Remember any from your childhood or grandparents?*

"*Isms*" such as racism, sexism, or ageism are another kind of bias. They discriminate against someone who differs in some real or imagined way from the biased person. They separate people and prevent close teamwork. Sexual harassment, when one gender offends the other by word or action, is also sexist. Harassment of any kind is wrong, morally and legally. The best leaders are *ism blind*. One way to ensure you are *ism blind* is by applying the Golden Rule in your relationships, treating others how you would want to be treated. This also means not playing favorites or using scapegoats.

Isms in the workplace are a sign of poor leadership and management. Try to be a role model free of them. It will help set a behavior standard that surpasses any written policy and will help others overcome their bias. With that kind of leadership there is higher morale and closer teamwork.

A word of caution: male leaders should not over-react to women and by doing so more attentive to their needs than male members (and, of course, vice versa). It is also important not to under-react and ignore sexually harassing males ("boys will be boys") or over-react with hyper-vigilance or by being overprotective (true for both genders).

SKILL BUILDER 10. Imagine yourself as supervisor in these situations. What would you do?
1. *While performing a task requiring physical strength a woman employee is having difficulty. What are the pros and cons of taking and not taking action? What kinds of action could you take?*
2. *A male worker tells a dirty joke. There are two women in the group. One smiles weakly but seems to you to be uncomfortable. The other woman blushes.*
3. *A male worker uses profanity at meetings and at his work station where there are men and women.*

NEEDS

Psychologist Abraham Maslow formulated a list of universal human needs. You should know and understand them because some can be met in the work situation. You can then help yourself and others realize them.

LEVEL 1: SURVIVAL

Air, food, and water and to be warm and dry, the universal dependency of infancy.

LEVEL 2: SECURITY

Shelter, safety, free from external danger, a need from early childhood.

LEVEL 3: SUPPORT

The "apron strings stage" of early and middle childhood and similar emotional support later.

LEVEL 4: SELF-ESTEEM
Fellow feeling, acceptance, belonging, team spirit, from teens to adulthood.

LEVEL 5: SELF-ACTUALIZATION
Personal fulfillment, achievement, realizing your potential.

In a serious accident, disaster, or under extreme stress, people at a high level are likely to function at a lower level. A person who has been at Level 4 may function at lower levels until the crisis has passed. This is common in wars and natural disasters. Sudden or increased stress such as being passed over for promotion, demoted, transferred, or fired can have a similar effect. Layoffs, downsizing, mergers, and takeovers are other factors that can cause a downward spiral to needs satisfaction.

SKILL BUILDER 11. *How do you, your department, and your company help workers meet need levels? How can you help yourself and those you work with and supervise meet these needs, especially the higher ones?*

UNMET NEEDS
Unmet needs can cause enough continued stress to lead to medical and psychological problems and they lower productivity. This can also be a sign of an inefficient organization and a need for change. So, unmet needs are important and you should be aware of them. When you see them, look for the cause. It could be personal, in you and your leadership style, in a worker, or both. It could be due to an organization's policies or procedures. If it's

organizational, take steps to help overcome it. If personal, check yourself out and adjust accordingly.

Often it helps to use a work group in shared decision-making rather than giving direct orders. This empowers workers with feelings of participation and responsibility and builds teamwork (*Skill 3*). Of course, there are times when direct leadership is best such as in an emergency, an impending deadline, or a decision involves information not available to the work group. Signs of unmet needs are high absenteeism, more frequent delays, inattention to detail, silences and withdrawing, distractions, apathy, cynicism or sarcasm, discouragement, depression, and high turnover.

SICK NEEDS

When needs are met inappropriately or excessively they become negative or sick. Power, sex, and money are drives that can push leaders to pursue needs to an extreme. They have corrupted many. Power changes people. It has been called intoxicating and even an aphrodisiac. Power is the major potentially corrupting drive. Money and sex are usually more available to people in power positions. As Lord Acton commented: "Power corrupts and absolute power corrupts absolutely."

Dr. Karen Horney (pronounced *horn eye*, please!) was an exceptional woman. Before World War 2 it was difficult for women to be admitted to medical school. She not only completed medical school but became a psychiatrist and was accepted by Freud for further training. That's quite an accomplishment. In her book *Neurosis and human growth* she lists ten needs that go to an unhealthy extreme:

1. *Excessive* affection and/or approval

2. *Excessive* (total) dependency
3. *Excessive* need to narrowly limit goals
4. *Excessive* power or control
5. *Excessive* need to exploit others
6. *Excessive* recognition or praise
7. *Excessive* need for personal admiration
8. *Excessive* need achievement and exclusivity
9. *Excessive* independence and self-sufficiency (no commitments)
10. *Excessive* need for perfection (invulnerability)

Note that the key word for each of these sick needs is ***excessive***. You may recognize a tendency toward some of these needs in yourself. A tendency is normal, an excess is not. They become abnormal, sick, when they are *excessive* and *extreme*. Leadership involves what may seem to others to be excessive needs but if they are in moderation they are normal. Leaders can be misunderstood because of their well-meaning but seemingly excessive drive. Dr. Horney listed six ways how personal effectiveness can be weakened:

1. *Relentless demands.* Examples: overachieving, seeing your best work as not good enough, or unrealistic expectations of others.

2. *Merciless self-accusation.* Examples: excessively blaming yourself for whatever goes wrong, exaggerated self-criticism.

3. *Self-contempt.* Examples: low self-concept and self-esteem. You really don't like yourself.

4. *High frustration level.* Examples: impatience, intolerance, overacting, having "a short fuse."

5. *Masochistic self-torment.* Examples: putting yourself down at every opportunity, failing to recognize and realize anything good you achieve.

6. *Self-destructive behavior.* Examples: pattern of failure in love, marriage, career, friendships; alcohol or drug abuse (including smoking); being accident prone.

SKILL BUILDER 12. How can you ensure your neurotic needs (if any) won't interfere with your leadership role and job performance? Think of examples of neurotic needs you have seen and use them as lessons of how not to behave. Observe TV personalities. Does their behavior suggest any neurotic needs?

SELF-ACTUALIZATION

Maslow studied successful well-adjusted people to find how they differed from others. He discovered personality traits he called *B-values* (B for becoming). They are healthy traits that bring self-actualization within reach. You and others *can* self-actualize in work, relationships, hobbies, and daily life, so it's important to be aware of them. The B-values are:

1. **Truth** rather than dishonesty, distrust, cynicism, or disbelief.
2. **Good, goodness** rather than evil, hate, selfishness, or negativism.
3. **Beauty, elegance** rather than ugliness, vulgarity, or being clumsy or shoddy.

4. **Unity, wholeness** rather than arbitrariness, useless nit-picking, or disorganization.
5. **Vitality, liveliness** rather than dull, empty, or an "emotionless robotism."
6. **Uniqueness** rather than monotony or lack of individuality.
7. **Completion** rather than imperfection, futility, or apathy.
8. **Order, orderliness** rather than chaos, tension, or disorder.
9. **Simplicity** rather than complexity, conflict, or confusion.
10. **Effortlessness,** "easy does it" rather than tedium, rigidity, or strain.
11. **Humor, playfulness** instead of being pretentious, stuffy, or distrusting.
12. **Self-sufficiency** rather than overdependence or insecurity.
13. **Meaning, meaningfulness** rather than emptiness, meaninglessness, or futility.
14. **Justice, fair play** rather than injustice, unfairness, or insecurity.

SKILL BUILDER 13. Reflect on each of the B-values. Rate yourself on a 3-point scale: 3 for high level, 2 for average but could use more, or 1 for low and needs much more. How can you maintain higher levels in your work and daily life?

PERSONALITY: YOURS AND THEIRS

Ralph Waldo Emerson once said: "Make the most of yourself, that's all there is of you!" Good advice! You should try to do your best and be the best you can be wherever you are, whatever you're doing. Personality is like that. It's *all there is of you*, "warts and all," strengths and weaknesses, natural talent and learned skills, attitude, mannerisms, and behavior. To better understand yourself you should have some knowledge of personality theory. There are many personality theories but four are basic and have inspired others:

1. BEHAVIORISM

Psychologist John Watson stated: "Give me a dozen healthy infants and my own specialized world and I'll train them to be doctor, lawyer, artist, merchant, and even beggar man or thief" (1925). He considered personality as *learned*, shaped by everything said and done to you since birth. John Locke saw the mind at birth as a blank slate. Russian physiologist Ivan Pavlov proved by experiments with dogs that behavior can be *conditioned*, a kind of learning. Dogs slobbered only to the sound of a bell that was previously rung only when meat was fed to them. B. F. Skinner showed how every-day behavior can be conditioned such as driving, un- locking doors, and using vending machines. Skinner proved personality development is mainly shaped by life experience. Others added *observational learning* (seeing then doing), and *modeling* yourself from those you admire.

Bottom line: Personality is shaped by learning and conditioning, trial and error, reward and punishment (the environment).

SKILL BUILDER 14. What aspects of your work and life reflect behaviorist principles? What are positive and negative aspects? How can you minimize any negatives?

2. PSYCHODYNAMIC THEORY (PSYCHOANALYSIS)

Sigmund Freud, a neurologist, described the mind as much like an iceberg, most of it out of sight below the surface, beyond reach of conscious awareness. That dark region holds secret wishes that surface only in dreams, with hypnosis, or in inadvertent slips of the tongue. He called it the unconscious. Like Watson, he saw behavior as motivated by pleasure avoiding pain but he disagreed it was due to learning and conditioning. Instead, Freud saw the prime motivator as instinct (heredity).

In his view, personality has three parts or states: the *superego* that functions as conscience, values, morals, and the ethical self; *id* functioning as "the beast within," the primitive, indulgent self; and *ego*, "the executive function" as mediator, manager, and data processor. The three states can be in conflict such as when overeating, drinking or smoking to excess. Then superego *shoulds* clash with id *craving*. The ego is stuck between them. A healthy ego mediates between the demands of the superego and id.

According to Freud, personality develops in five phases: oral at birth and through infancy (nursing, kissing); anal at about age 2 (toileting); phallic in parent-child sex role conflict (Oedipus complex, castration fear, penis envy); latency from age 7 to puberty (mainly physical growth without sexual aspects); and genital from puberty onward (appropriate gender behavior). There is evidence in everyday conversation that Freud was right: "That sucks...pain in the butt...all screwed up."

Bottom line: You are more of an animal than you realize. Personality is influenced by basic instinctive drives (heredity).

SKILL BUILDER 15. What aspects of your work and life reflect Freud's theory? What are the positive and negative aspects? How can you minimize any negatives?

3. HUMANISTIC PSYCHOLOGY

According to Watson, you are the victim of circumstances, whatever happens to you from birth. To Freud, your life is like a card game, dealt a hand of instinctive drives at birth and stuck with it. Neither conceded that heredity (nature) or environment (nurture) could be overcome. But history is full of examples of gifted people who overcame shortcomings. Examples are Beethoven's deafness when he composed the stirring 9th symphony, the blind Homer and Helen Keller, and Franklin Roosevelt's polio. You can probably think of more.

A "third force" emerged as a reaction to the fatalism and determinism of Freud and Watson: humanistic psychology. Carl Rogers was one of its leaders. He emphasized the value of empathy and unconditional positive regard for others. Abraham Maslow was another leader in this human potential movement. He began his career as a behaviorist but chose the humanistic model because of his studies of successful people. This led him to see personality as not fixed but continually *becoming*, a journey more than a destination. He isolated and explained the B-values of becoming and the signs of self-actualization. Great art, music, and literature are consistent with humanistic psychology.

Transpersonal psychology is a more recent development, reflected in alternative and holistic medicine or wellness. Ancient Asian sources are used such as Buddhism, Tai Chi and yoga exercises, meditation, and guided imagery,

Bottom line: Negative factors of environment and heredity can be transcended by will power, intelligence, and ingenuity to *self-actualize* yourself.

SKILL BUILDER 16. What aspects of your work and life reflect humanistic principles? How would they affect your leadership style positively and negatively? How can you minimize any negatives and maximize the positives?

4. TRAITS AND TYPES

This is the oldest personality theory, dating back at least to 300 BCE to Hippocrates. He was a priest-physician of the ancient Greek Cult of Asklepios who practiced on the island of Kos. Medical doctors today still take "the Hippocratic Oath" in which they "swear by Apollo" to administer to the sick. Terms he used to describe illness are still standards: acute or chronic, and mild, moderate, or severe. He described four personality types, each with specific traits: sanguine (energetic, optimistic); choleric (irritable, nagging); phlegmatic (passive, withdrawn), or melancholic (moody, depressed). Pavlov found that the dogs he used in his experiments fell into four behavior types.

Psychiatrist Carl Jung described three personality traits, each on a scale between extremes (extraversion-introversion; thinking-feeling; and sensing-intuiting).

Isabel Myers Briggs added a fourth: judging-perceiving. To take a self-test to detect where you fall on these scales check the *Keirsey Temperament Sorter* in the references at the end of this chapter. Psychology's latest personality theory is *5-factor theory*. It is based on an analysis of all previously reported traits and types that were narrowed down to five basic traits:

1. **Emotional stability:** overall mental health, calm more than anxious, feeling secure more than insecure, enough self-confidence to cope well with stress.
2. **Extraversion**: Outgoing and friendly, enjoy being with people, and sharing and showing feelings easily.
3. **Openness** to new ideas and experiences, to change, fantasy, and being more imaginative than practical, curious and explorative, usually with an artistic flair.
4. **Agreeableness:** Cooperative, caring, more helpful and trusting than not, honest, straightforward, and often modest.
5. **Conscientiousness:** Organized, careful, diligent, reliable, and self-disciplined.

Bottom line: Be aware of your traits and maximize the positive, minimize the negatives.

SKILL BUILDER 17. If the five factors were the qualifications for promotion, how would you score on them? Rate yourself 1 for fair, 2 for average, and 3 for above average. In which trait are you strongest? Weakest? What can you do to function at higher levels in all five areas?

SKILL BUILDER 18. *Which theory do you feel best describes human nature? Why? What does your choice tell you about yourself? All four continue to be listed in psychology textbooks, evidence they are useful models of behavior. Eliminate any the dynamics of personality would be incomplete.*

BUILDING SELF-CONFIDENCE
BE A GOOD KISSER!

KISS is an acronym for the common sense advice: *Keep It Simple, Sweetheart* (let's drop *Stupid*, the usual last word, since it's a put-down and we choose to be positive). To KISS means avoiding doubletalk, jargon, and technical language. It *is* possible to simplify complex subjects. There are leaders who are *simplifiers* and those who are *complicators, lumpers* and *splitters*. Which are you? How good a *KISSer* are you, really? To find out, do this *Skill Builder:*

SKILL BUILDER 19. *Read the following paragraph then summarize it in one simple sentence. The answer is at the end of this chapter (don't peek!).*

> Human perceptual processing varies considerably both phylogenetically and idiosyncratically, subject to both intrinsic and extrinsic variables. Genetic endowment and predisposition are intrinsic variables and situation-specific phenomena such as figure-ground, relative illumination, and operative distracting environmental cues are extrinsic variables. Either or both extrinsic and intrinsic factors obfuscate the differential dis-

crimination of visual stimuli. Ornithic behavior offers a heuristic example, where an avian species member of special interest eludes closer scrutiny and identification by classificatory schema. Experience confirms it is practicable to focus attention on one typical specimen tactually rather than by secondary visual attention of others of the same or similar species.

THINK ON YOUR FEET

The ability to think on your feet and speak "off the cuff" (extemporaneously) is a positive leadership trait. It is the ability to speak comfortably with little or no preparation, notes, or script. It's been called "having good stage presence." Try the next skill builder to test your informal speaking skill.

SKILL BUILDER 20. Write numerals from 1 to 12 on separate strips of paper. Fold them, mix them up, then pick one. Read it aloud then take two minutes to talk about it and agree or disagree with it. Discard that paper and pick another or pick one a day and have 12 days to practice different subjects. Try recording your voice. Notice your choice of words, rate of speech, voice tone, and clarity. A good way to avoid "uh" and "er" is by using pauses instead (also helps you keep relaxed).
1. *Old is better than new*
2. *City living beats country living*
3. *Winter is better than summer*
4. *Beef is better than fish*
5. *Hunting is better than fishing*
6. *Renting is better than owning*

7. *Leasing* is better than *owning* a car
8. Living in the North is better than living in the South.
9. *Coffee* is better than *tea*
10. Being *conservative* is better than being *liberal.*
11. *Driving* is better than *flying.*
12. Being a *woman* is better than being a *man.*

SPEAK UP

Some say good speakers are born, not made. *Not true!* Effective speaking is a skill that can be learned, polished, and perfected. Every talk has three parts. Here they are with suggestions:

1. **Opener***:* Best with a joke, a shared confidence (be judicious!), current event, prop, etc.
2. **Body***:* outline your key points, underline or highlight them or put key words in large print. Best with human interest angle. Use notes only to stay on track – never read them.
3. **Close***:* summarize, with a snappy end.

SUGGESTIONS
1. Dress appropriately, not too flashy or too casual.
2. Follow the old preacher's advice: "Tell'em what yer gonna tell'em. Tell'em. Then tell'em what you told'em."
3. Begin by getting audience attention. Keep jokes short.
4. Look at the audience (between heads if nervous).
5. Check the room for echo and volume needed. Hold or adjust a microphone a few inches from your mouth.
6. Ask anyone with a question to wait until you're finished (or you may not have time to finish).

7. Don't read or memorize but rehearsing aloud or mentally helps.
8. Don't mumble. Articulate words clearly.
9. Keep your head up. Don't bury your nose!
10. Pause and be silent instead of "uh, er, mmm, like, y'know, y'unnerstand."
11. Use good pacing and tim*ing*, not too fast nor too slow. Watch TV to learn from actors, actresses, reporters, talk show hosts, and their guests.
12. Use gestures *only* if they're natural, never forced.
13. Never hold up a poster or graph. Tape it (sturdily), hang it, or ask someone to hold it up and in clear view.
14. Anything printed on a poster or chart should be readable by the audience – even in the last row.
15. Establish a psychological and emotional bond with the audience. Signs of good bonding are audience laughter at jokes, active response to questions asked, smiles or nods. Bad signs are audience looking down or away, talking, yawning -- or walking out.

SKILL BUILDER 21. Read a newspaper editorial and think how you would elaborate, agree or disagree with it. Do it aloud. In the same way, react to a TV news commentator or talk show guest. What you can do to improve your speaking effectiveness?

WRITE RIGHT

What you write is what you think and so it should read the same as what you would have said. What you write is also a projection of your personality and leadership style.

The sign of good writing is when others comment reading it was like hearing you speak the words. You are judged by what you write. Poor writing makes a poor impression. There are many times when your only contact with others is in writing. For these reasons you should consider writing skills a high priority.

USE THE THREE C's

1. CLARITY. Use understandable language. Consider these *unclear* statements:
(a) *The missing manager was found by the bar.*
   Bars don't find anyone.
(b) *After eating, the van left for the office.*
   Vans don't eat.
(c) *The owner opened the store and was shot in the rear.*
   Shot in a part of the body or building?

Readability is an important part of writing clearly. What good is what you write if no one understands it? Be aware of the reading level of those who will read what you write. Comic books are written at a 6th grade reading level. News magazines are at the 11th grade level. There are several methods of measuring reading level and you may find it helpful to use one to check your writing. One of the simplest and more recent is the *Fry Reading Guide* (1977).

2. Be **CONCISE**. William Strunk, author of the most used style manual, maintained "a sentence should contain no unnecessary words and a paragraph no unnecessary sentence." This is called a journalistic style and its major feature is word economy. A handy rule: *If in doubt leave it out.*

3. Be **CORRECT**. Misspelllings and poor usage suggest sloppy, hurried thinking. Other common errors are: too many commas, *which* instead of *that* (try deleting *that* to see if it makes any difference – it seldom does); jargon or technical language (KISS it!); and too many acronyms ("The IRS didn't OK my 1040 so I was SOL"). Part of being correct is being *authentic*, real, yourself, and not phony or imitating anyone.

SKILL BUILDER 22. Randomly pick samples of your writing from the file (letters, memos, policies, etc. Scan them for unnecessary word usage, misspellings, and awkward usage. Do you use the same style and wording for superiors as for subordinates or entry-level workers? It helps to have someone else review them for you for the three C's. Most writing could be shorter, in simple sentences and understandable wording. As you read newspapers and magazines, think of how the writing could be improved, or if well written, how you can use the same style to improve your writing.

IMPROVE YOUR MEMORY

Ever been embarrassed talking to someone whose name you can't remember? A good memory is an asset personally and professionally. It is easier to remember names and details by linking them to something you already know. *Mnemonics* (say "nee-mon-icks") is a way to improve memory by linking names or numbers to mental images of them such as Archer, Bell, Carpenter, or Weaver. A series of numbers can be remembered by linking words to them, the sillier the better: "two dirty sticks" for 236. Imaginary situations can be used: "office hours 7 to 6" for 726, "two for tea" for 240, "seven won 98 dollars" for 7198, "too ate late" for 288, or "nine visitors went to see two six sicks" for 92C266.

Another memory aid is *rehearsal,* going over what you want to remember as you hear it, repeating it silently to yourself several times. **Recitation** is doing it aloud, like kids learning the alphabet. **Chunking** is breaking down information into smaller bits or groups by similar or dissimilar features, prioritizing by what's most important, outlining or using checklists or columns to simplify the information. Some people use their own personal shorthand or abbreviations to chunk data.

SKILL BUILDER 23. Using your last name or of people at work, in your family or neighborhood, think of possible mnemonics to remember them. Test your skill at coming up with mnemonics by taking names from TV news, programs, or movies. Try to do this daily.

FIGHT BURNOUT!

Burnout is physical and/or emotional exhaustion from continued unvented stress. The antidote is to fight it. If you don't, like swimming in an alligator infested swamp, *it will eat you*! Some stress is unavoidable and research shows can be a good tonic for mind and body. George Bernard Shaw said he'd "rather wear out than rust out." If stress continues or increases without being vented or lessened, burnout risk also increases and can lead to serious medical or mental problems. Signs of burnout:

Physical: fatigue, disturbed sleep, increased or decreased appetite, startle response (being jumpy), and psychosomatic disorders.

Emotional: irritability, mood swings, anxiety and/or depression, feeling helpless, disillusioned, or discouraged.

Psychological: Personality or behavior change, social withdrawal, depersonalization ("I'm not myself...this is not me" or others tell you "you don't seem to be yourself"), or derealization ("This isn't happening...it's unreal").

Spiritual: Feelings of meaninglessness, emptiness, fatalistic attitude.

GENERAL ADAPTATION SYNDROME

Hans Selye spent decades studying animals and humans under stress. In his book *The stress of life* he described a 3-phase process of burnout he called the *General Adaptation Syndrome* or GAS. He found that regardless of the type of stress, the effect as the same and always in three stages:

1. **Alarm** This is the arousal phase. Heart and breathing rate increase. Anxiety level is higher than usual. You "feel stressed."
2. **Resistance.** Anxiety seems to decrease because the body adjusted to it but often unnoticed are changes in body chemistry. The body's immune system weakens, lowering resistance to disease.
3. **Exhaustion.** This is the final and most dangerous phase. Body chemistry and organ systems can reach life-threatening potential. Death can be the result!

Other researchers confirm a downward spiral from continued unvented stress. Edelwich and Brodsky describe a 4-stage stage process in their book *Burnout*. Each stage is like a fork in the road where you have a choice of which way to go. Sometimes the choice is not a conscious process and circumstances and problems move you to either of these choices:

Enthusiasm or *realism,* then to
Activity or *stagnation,* then to
Satisfaction or *frustration,* then to
Involvement or *apathy.*

In an article entitled *Characteristics of burnout,* Pines and Maslach describe burnout effect as levels in a downward spiral:

Emotional exhaustion leads to
Cynicism and insensitivity leads to
Low self concept ("I'm a total failure").

SKILL BUILDER 24. Have you experienced any of these stress stages or phases? Did you do anything to minimize them? Continue to be aware of them so you can take steps to reduce their effect.

SOME SUGGESTIONS
1. *Recognize and accept limits*. Do the best you can, then let go.
2. *Prioritize.* Change the order of doing things to avoid boredom. Keeps you fresh.
3. *Bite the bullet.* Don't put off disagreeable tasks. They get heavier when delayed.

4. *Choose to be positive.* Find something positive in any negative situation.
5. *Tolerate and forgive.* Don't carry extra baggage. It clutters the mind.
6. Use stressful situations to *inoculate* you against future stress, using better ways to cope the next time.
7. *Vent* outside the office (jog, walk, wash the car, garden, putter, listen to music, get a hobby).
8. *Learn to relax more,* to really let go, to find and enjoy a childlike, dog/cat-nap space. Consider learning how to meditate or do Tai Chi.
9. *Have fun.* Laugh more. Find something funny every day or do something funny yourself. Be a kid again.
10. *Take care of yourself* with exercise, eating sensibly, and with regular medical checkups. Don't smoke. Drink in moderation.

SKILL BUILDER 25. How many of those suggestions have you been following? Which are you not following? Is it possible for you to follow all ten? If so, exert a conscious effort to do so. Schedule them if you must.

MINISCRIPTS

Everyone has a *miniscript* according to therapist Taibi Kahler. It's like a tape that plays automatically in your head with a message (*miniscript*) the instant something goes wrong. Kahler estimated that by age five you've heard 25,000 hours of these messages from parents or other authority figures. These "must messages" get summarized in your mind as *miniscript drivers.* There are five of thermo:

> I must *try harder*
> I must *be perfect*
> I must *be strong*
> I must *hurry*
> I must *please him/her/them/myself*

Whatever goes wrong *hooks* one or more drivers. If not neutralized the message is amplified into a *stopper* message:
> I *failed again*!
> I *could/should have done better*!
> I *really let him/her/them/myself down*!

The resulting feeling is *I'm not OK but you're OK*. If not neutralized a *stopper* pushes you down even more to **Final Miniscript Position** (FMP): *I'm not OK, you're not OK, and nothing is OK*. This can lead to alcohol or drug abuse, divorce, getting fired, even suicide. The antidote is to neutralize a *driver* the instant it's "hooked." This is done with a memorized automatic *allower* such as:
> It's OK *to make a mistake sometimes*
> It's OK *to do and not overdo*
> It's OK *to take care of myself*!
> It's OK *to be me* (or write your own!)

The most effective way to use *allowers* is to match them to the *driver* you hear most frequently. Most people hear one or two more than others. Memorize *allowers* so you hear them the instant a *driver* is heard. It can help to post them at the phone, desk, or refrigerator so they're visible immediately and help you keep them in mind.

SKILL BUILDER 26. What are your most frequent <u>drivers</u>? List them in priority order, from the one heard most often. Which <u>allower</u> would best neutralize it or others? Type or clearly write the <u>allower</u> on an index card or post-it note and put it where you are most likely to be hooked by your <u>drivers</u>. Learn to match the <u>allower</u> to the <u>driver</u> instantly when it "plays" in your head. In time you'll be able to neutralize drivers automatically.

THE ZEN OF LEADERSHIP

Zen Buddhism dates back to the 5th century in China. One of its teachings is *satori*, an instant flash of insight, like the "Ahah" of Archimedes when the solution of a problem suddenly came to him. Insight can come suddenly like that or slowly over time. You can experience it as you study leadership skills. Something you thought you knew may not be so. Something you didn't know may come in an "Ahah" moment of enlightenment.

Another Zen method is teaching in a parable or story with an inner hook toward a flash of insight. One parable is that of a young man anxious to learn Zen who visits a Zen master. See if it flashes for you:

YOUNG MAN: I'm so happy to meet you. I can be with you once or twice a week until I have learned Zen. How long would it take?

MASTER: That would take more than a year.

YOUNG MAN: I don't have that much time. What if I met with you every day?

MASTER: That would take two years.

YOUNG MAN: Oh, but what if I became your servant and was with you every day and every night and studied especially hard. How long then?

MASTER: Then it would take three years.
YOUNG MAN (bewildered): I don't understand. Why would it take so much longer if I'm with you more?
MASTER: Because a person in such a hurry learns very slowly.

Get it? With Zen, sometimes it flashes for you and sometimes it doesn't. What the Zen master was teaching is it takes time to learn and master any subject. Leadership skills are like that. Just reading this book isn't enough. You have to experience the lessons, what in the East they call "being one with it." Absorb the meaning, let it incubate in you, and it will become "second nature," immediately useful. A sign of developing leadership skill is the ability to apply it spontaneously as needed. As this happens you will know you're on your way to becoming not only the best you but also an effective leader. In the words of an old Zen proverb: "When the apple is ripe, it drops from the tree of its own weight." Leadership skills emerge when ripe, after study, thought, and practice.

KEEPING WELL

To support and help others, you need to be in good physical and mental health. Here are 15 ways to keep well, feel fit, positive, and healthy physically and mentally:

1. **Be yourself – and get excited about it!**
   Accept yourself for who and what you are and do the best you can. Ralph Waldo Emerson once said: "Make the most of yourself. That's all there is of you."
2. **Recognize and accept limits**
   Do all you can and when you can and when you can do no more *let go of it!*

3. **Prioritize**
   Re-arrange your schedule to keep fresh. Do a disagreeable task first, while you're fresh.
4. **Schedule worry times**
   Like 5 or 10 minutes a day and no more. Worrying continually wears you down. There is no discount from a bill worrying about it.
5. **Be positive**
   Consciously, deliberately, choose to be positive. Find something positive in any negative situation. End the day remembering and reflecting on one positive thing that happened.
6. **Tolerate and forgive**
   Don't carry the extra baggage of unfinished mental business.
7. **Be a matador**
   Sidestep the charging bull of someone's anger or frustration. Remind yourself that you choose not to be the target. *It* (the problem), or *he* or *she* is the problem (the bull), so side step it. Don't be the target.
8. **Use stress as an inoculation**
   Learn from it using it to develop better coping skills for the next time and you will grow stronger with every setback. This is an idea of Canadian psychologist Don Meichenbaum.
9. **Vent!**
   Learn to "get it out of your system" with a **contract partner** or by gardening, washing the car, jogging, walking, listening to relaxing music, etc. You **contract** with a person you trust to share personal concerns. It's a contract because both of you agree beforehand to join together to help each other grow personally.

10. **Take care of your body**
    Exercise. Have good nutrition. Try eating slower, a little less if necessary, cutting up food in smaller pieces, and take a moment more to enjoy the taste. Don't smoke!
11. **Take timeouts**
    Go on mini-vacations and take fun breaks. You need and deserve them! **Get away** in a garden, church or temple, a library, park bench, or comfy chair.
12. **Learn to do nothng – exceptionally well**
    Relax *totally* in that calm, unhurried infant or dog/cat nap OK feeling. Enjoy it more often.
13. **Laugh more**
    Notice something funny every day. If you can't find anything funny, do something silly yourself! Read the comics, watch more comedies, and share jokes.
14. **Be a kid more**
    Hug the *Eternal Child* inside you. When's the last time you had an ice cream cone? Chewed bubble gum and popped a big bubble?
15. **Get a hobby**
    Find a hobby that's more physical than mental, more restful than tedious.

SKILL BUILDER 27. *How many of these wellness tips do you use? Which do you especially like? Enjoy them more! Which are you not doing? Why not? Try the ones you like.*

SKILL BUILDER 28. Review this chapter and reflect on the material. This first skill is important, because it must rest on a firm, stable foundation and only you can build it. Before you go on to Skill 2, be sure you understand and can apply the material. If any of it is not clear, read it again. If you would like to study any of it further, check out any of the useful references (below) at a large public library. If they are not available there, check a used book website entering author and title.

REALIZE SKILL 1 !

After each of the four basic skills there is a parting thought to help you realize that skill. To help you realize the fist skill there are two bits of advice. The first is from Ralph Waldo Emerson:

> **Make the most of yourself**
> **-- that's all there is of you.**

The second is "the Alaska sourdough's credo." Use it to look back, year to year, to check how you have grown personally and professionally:

> **I ain't what I wanna be;**
> **I ain't what I'm gonna be,**
> **but I sure as hell**
> **ain't what I used to be!**

ANSWER TO "LEARN TO KISS"

A simple sentence that summarizes the meaning of the paragraph: *A bird in the hand is worth two in the bush.*

FOR FURTHER STUDY

On self-awareness

Cross, J., & Cross, P.B. *Knowing yourself inside out.* Berkeley CA: Crystal Publications, 1998.

Drucker, P. *The daily Drucker: 366 days of insight and motivation for getting things done.* New York: Harper-Collins, 2003.

Keirsey, D., & Bates, M. *Please understand me: Character and temperament types.* Del Mar CA: Prometheus Nemesis Books, 1978.

Maslow, A.H. *The farther reaches of human nature.* New York: Viking, 1971.

Feist, J. *Theories of personality.* New York: Harcourt Brace, 1994.

Horney, K. *Neurosis and human growth.* New York: Norton, 1950.

Maslow, A.H. *Toward a psychology of being.* Princeton NJ: Van Nostrand, 1968.

Maslow, A.H. *Motivation and personality.* New York: Harper and Row, 1970.

McClelland, D.C. *Human motivation.* Glenview IL: Scott Foresman, 1985.

O'Hanlon, W. *Taproots.* New York: Norton, 1987.

About gender

Bem, S.L. *The lenses of gender.* New Haven CT: Yale University Press, 1993.

Gilligan, C. *In a different voice: Psychological theory and women's development.* Cambridge MA: Harvard University Press, 1982.

Gilligan, C., Lyons, P., & Hanmer, T.J. *Making connections.* Cambridge MA: Harvard University Press, 1990.

Sax, L. *Why gender matters.* New York: Doubleday, 2005.

Tavris, C. *The mismeasure of woman.* New York: Simon and Schuster, 1992.

About burnout

Edelwich, J., & Brodsky, A. *Burnout: Stages of disillusionment.* New York: Human Sciences Press, 1980.

Kahler, T. *Transactional analysis revisited.* Little Rock AR: Human Development Publishing, 1978.

Pines, A., & Maslach, C. (1978). Characteristics of burnout in mental health settings. *Hospital and Community Psychiatry,* 29, 233-237, 1978.

Selye, H. *The stress of life.* New York: McGraw-Hill, 1956.

Peale, N.V. *The power of positive thinking.* P.O. Box 8000, Pawling, NY 12566

SKILL 2

WHO ARE THESE OTHER PEOPLE?
Interpersonal awareness

There can be no leaders without followers. To be accepted and to succeed leaders must motivate, even inspire their followers. It is not possible to do so unless leaders understand others. As **Skill 1** made clear, you can't really understand others until you understand yourself. Before you read further, skim through **Skill 1** to ensure you have a good understanding of that material. If you don't, it can limit your ability to fully understand and apply the ideas and techniques of **Skill 2**.

LISTENING SKILLS: THE ARC METHOD

ARC stands for each letter of a listening skill which, if used regularly, can prevent misunderstanding:

- A is being **ATTENTIVE**, alert to and aware of what is said.

- R is **REFLECTION**, mirroring what is said

- C is **CLARIFICATION**, ensuring what's said is clearly understood

A
ATTENTIVE

This first step sets the stage for effective listening. It is having an open, receptive, attitude, without judging or concluding, just waiting to hear what will be said. It is like tuning a radio to a set frequency but not yet hearing anything. Everyone has a right to an opinion, even a right to be wrong. The goal is to hear what is said, not what you want to hear or would like to hear. A sign of this step is ng *following behavior*: a nod, eye contact, a slight smile, leaning a bit toward the speaker, or acknowledging words such as "Uh-uh...yes... I see what you mean... I understand...sounds like...I hear you saying..." etc.

R
REFLECTION

This step is the most frequently omitted and when it is it almost always results in misunderstanding. The goal is *not* to react to what has been said, *not* to debate, agree or disagree, but to show you understand by reflecting back (like a mirror) what has been said *in your own words*. Signs of this step are neutral body language (especially face and eyes), neutral tone of voice and choice of words ("I hear you saying...") or your own *neutral* response). Avoid asking "do you mean...are you saying...do I understand you to be saying..." These statements can sound antagonistic.

C
CLARIFICATION

The goal of this step is acknowledging and if needed, refining what was said *still without taking sides*. It's a final assurance the intended message has been understood. The speaker accepts or corrects the reflection of the listener. After clarification both sides can agree, differ, or discuss the matter further.

SKILL BUILDER 29. *If in a group or with a friend or coworker, pair off for a timed 2-minute interaction. One e person reads then continues a sentence stem (below). The other person reflects then the original speaker clarifies. Time limit: one minute each. Then switch roles and for one minute the original listener finishes the same sentence stem which is reflected by the original speaker (now listener), and clarified. In groups, change partners for each sentence stem so there is interaction with five different people.*
1. *When meeting someone for the first time, I feel...* **(finish the statement).**
2. *What I look for and need in a friend is ...*
3. *What I like about this company is . . .*
4. *What I dislike about this company is . . .*
5. *What I think about this ARC system is . . .*

THE JOHARI WINDOW

The *Johari window* is a model of poor communications developed by Joseph Luft and Harry Ingham. It is a line drawing of a square with intersecting vertical and horizontal lines to look like a 4-paned window. Each pane is a square of the same length and width. The four panes are identified as: **What we know** (upper left), **What only I know** (upper right), **What only you know** (lower left), and **Unknown to both of us** (lower right).

It is a graphic way to show poor communication because the area unknown to you and me are as large as the areas of what each of us knows. What both know is only as large as our individual areas. Such a situation might not cause trouble where individuals work alone, such as college faculties, research scientists, doctors, or lawyers. But, in most firms it's important to share knowledge and expertise, experience and techniques, and the only way to expand *we know* is to collaborate and share what everyone knows. Those lines move down and to the right, enlarging *we know* and reduce the *unknown*. The ideal is to have the largest possible *we know* space. There will still be small *unknown, I know* and *you know* spaces because it isn't possible for anyone to know *everything* another person knows. In the closest-knit team, a human relationship, or even in the most "together" person there is a small area of unknown. Don't let it worry you. Know-it-alls are a pain -- mainly because they know so little! Their verbal smoke screen conceals their insecurity and fear they don't really know it all.

SKILL BUILDER 30. How equal are your window panes? How can you decrease the unknown and help others do the same? Make notes to yourself to remind you to work on improving your interpersonal communications.

CONGRUENCE: GET IT TOGETHER

Virginia Satir was a marriage and family therapist who developed a useful model of personal communication she called *congruence*, being together, unified, in agreement. It means you "have it all together," you're "with it," and "tuned in." It's another way to check the relative efficiency of communication *within yourself* as well as between you and another person, you and your company, department, team, and coworkers. Two circles are used. One represents one person and what that person knows. The second circle represents another person and what that person knows. As the circles intersect, a new area of overlap between them shows what they know together. Congruence is how closely the circles coincide, like spotlights on a stage. The more they converge, the greater the congruence between them. There is *no* communication if the circles don't touch at all. If they just overlap a bit, congruence is low and communication is poor.

Optimal communication is when the circles overlap so much they almost appear as one. It is not possible to have a perfect fit. The best you can expect is two circles with just a bit of each on one side and the other. What's left out is the private or personal space of the individual, an area not open because there isn't enough time or opportunity for sharing, or it isn't relevant or needed. The two circles of congruence can be used to show how "together" your thoughts and feelings are or your self-awareness and awareness of others. How congruent are a company's goals or policies and its actual performance and procedures.

SKILL BUILDER 31. How congruent are you? How do your circles of self-awareness (intra-personal awareness) and awareness of others (interpersonal awareness) intersect? What can you do for a better fit? What do your company's circles of policy and procedure look like? What can be done for a better fit?

BODY LANGUAGE

Body language, nonverbal communication or *kinesics*, is the way posture, placement, and movements show attitude, thoughts, and feelings. Right now, at this instant, stop reading and be aware of your body placement and posture. Standing or sitting? Legs crossed? Sitting upright or reclining? Observe your own body language. What does it show about what you are thinking or feeling? Whether you are relaxed or bored, interested or impatient, your body sends signals.

A word of caution: you can read too much in another person's body language but it is also possible to miss some important and useful clues. Some people have certain favorite ways of sitting, standing, and even walking. You may be showing this right now. Someone can feel anxious but appear relaxed and not "on the edge of the chair." Still, there are some generalizations that are valid. Body language can be

... *learned* from parents, others, or yourself as a habit

... a *reflex*, like a startle reaction or eye blink. Some people are naturally "jumpy,"

... *conscious choice* such as waving, pointing, or shrugging,

... *role behavior* like directing someone or a cop directing traffic.

A 5-year-old greeted his dad returning home from work with: "Watch out for Mom, she's mad." Asked how he knew that, the lad replied: "She's mad 'cause she *walks* mad." It *is* possible to make valid generalizations about someone's mood from their body language. If you're very tired you probably *walk tired* with more of a shuffle than usual. Your eye contact may also be less direct. Books on body language tend to over-generalize and it's best to have more evidence of a person's mood or thoughts before making a conclusion.

It can take years of marriage for a couple to really read each other's unspoken thoughts or feelings. One book suggests a person is irritated when arms are folded, psychological distance or even hostility if a leg is crossed against another person as if defending against that person. Some people feel comfortable sitting with legs crossed regardless of anyone sitting next to them. Others find crossing their arms relaxing.

Before concluding anything other factors should be considered such as verbal and nonverbal behaviors and what you know about the person. See what's there, not what you want to see or would like to see. Human behavior is complex. Don't oversimplify or jump to conclusions. With that word of caution, here are the specific features of body language:

Position and posture, *where* and *how* you sit, stand, and walk

Place behavior such as at a party, in church, at the beach, in a library, school, restaurant, etc.

Personal space, the physical distance between you, pets, kids, friends, coworkers, boss, others.

Gesture, *signals* given by hand or finger(s).

Incidence, *how often* it happens.

Intensity and range of motion, the *force* of movement and *how great a distance covered.*

Face and head signals, involvement of forehead, eyebrows, eyelids, eyes, mouth, lips, tongue, cheeks (the most accurate according to experts) .

Costume: Uniform or clothing, its design, color, and fit.

Ornamentation: Rings, pins, tattoos

Props: Tools, clipboard, briefcase, files, forms, book, etc.

SKILL BUILDER 32. Without being obvious, observe the body language of others in specific situations.

Notice how some mannerisms can be accurate but sometimes misleading. Be aware of your own body language. Be careful not to give any false signals or betray what you're really feeling when it wouldn't be wise to do so.

VERBAL DEFENSES

In stressful situations that are beyond our control we sometimes cope by using *defense mechanisms*. They come from the part of the mind Freud called the unconscious, below conscious awareness. They are automatic, like a boxer with his guard up defending against a blow that might come at any moment. Psychological defenses are like that. We are unaware we use them until someone points it out or you become aware yourself by over-reacting in a situation. Here's a list of defense mechanisms you may see, in yourself as well as in others:

1. **Acting out** is impulsive behavior such as losing self-control and over-reacting with an outburst of temper, angrily walking out, swearing, or trashing things.
2. **Avoidance** is refusal or inability to acknowledge a problem by:

    Denial, failing to take personal responsibility for obvious reactions or attitude such as loudly exclaiming: "Who's angry? Not me!" or a tearful "Oh, that's all right, it was nothing" when it *is* something really upsetting.

    Suppression, a *conscious choice* to avoid a problem, person, or situation. Example: Scarlett O'Hara (Vivien Leigh) in the movie *Gone with the Wind* Saying: "Tomorrow's another day." She admitted she had a problem but chose not to deal with it.

3. **Externalization** is blaming others or other circumstances for your own shortcomings, such as: "If it weren't for (you or it) I would have gotten it done." Variations:

   Displacement, *dumping* anger or frustration on someone or something not involved in the problem or situation. Also called *flypaper syndrome* since you stick it on someone or something else rather than getting at the real problem cause;

   Isolation, "nit picking" by exaggerating a minor problem, "making a mountain out of a molehill." It is also rushing to judgment with too few facts. "Air bags are dangerous because they kill babies." Doing away with them would kill many more men, women, and children than the infants who died from them;

   Projection, like shining a flashlight (projecting) onto others, falsely blaming them for your own thoughts or feelings. "That office spends too much time socializing" might mean "Why can't we have fun like that, too?"

4. **Exaggeration** is *distorting* reality, by:

   Discounting or **devaluing** is putting down someone or something or badmouthing a person or problem.

   Idealization, halo effect, is exaggerating a person's positive behaviors or traits out of realistic proportion, such as hero worship and fan clubs. It's normal to admire people and consider them role models but not exaggerate their positive qualities so much no one could equal them.

5. **Humor** is a healthy defense to casually brush away embarrassment or lighthearted needling. Used

positively it is an effective icebreaker, helps overcome distance, and draws people together. It is negative and destructive when used to avoid reality, hurt others, or distance you from a problem or reality.
6. **Smoke screen** is defending yourself by "blowing smoke" in words or actions that confuse and keep people at a distance. There are two kinds:
   Intellectualizing, double talk, word salad, head tripping, or **"BS"** is launching into technical jargon or abstract ideas, trivia or tangents with little or no real meaning.
   Rationalizing is explaining away a problem. Robert Louis Stevenson said: "I've heard many excuses but not one good reason."
7. **Passive-aggressive behavior, foot dragging, dogging it, sandbagging,** and being a **passive obstructionist,** is as the saying goes: "You can lead a horse to water but you can't make it drink." Example: Not attending a meeting when an important issue is to be discussed.

SKILL BUILDER 33. Have you heard any of these defense mechanisms at home or on the job? How many do you use? While they become automatic you can learn to use more constructive behaviors in stressful situations and feel more comfortable you no longer need them.

INTERACTING AND TRANSACTING

SKILL BUILDER 34. There are three parts to this exercise. They will be explained after you do them.
1. Think of something you should be doing but aren't, a "must" or "should" message you're giving yourself.

Don't explain or discuss it, just say it.
2. *Imagine the world is divided in half, a world of thinking and a world of feeling. In such a world where would you live (e.g., 60-40 think-feel, 20-80 thinking-feeling, etc.)*
3. *Recall a happy childhood memory, something you did as a child that was a happy experience for you.*

YOUR THREE EGO STATES

Skill Builder 34 was designed to "hook" each of three different parts of you that co-exist in your personality. They are accessible to you and others at any time, in any situation. Depending on the circumstances or the relationship, one of the three parts will be involved more than the others. The three parts are: **Parent** (capitalized because it isn't your real-life parent but a parent-like state of mind inside you); **Child**; and **Adult**. Let's take a closer look at them:

PARENT (+ and –)

This part of you "comes on" at about age 5, like a tape that plays automatically with messages of what you *must, should, or ought to be doing*. Your *Parent* has two sides, the positive or *+ Parent* and the negative or *- Parent*.

Your *+ Parent* is the caring parent force within you. It is accepting, approving, and supportive, and is the source of values, ethics, and morals. **Verbal clues:** "Well done...good...nice..." **Body language:** Pat, thumbs up, smile, approving nod.

Your *- Parent* is the critical parent within you, blaming, strict, over-controlling, opinionated, cruel, and punitive. **Verbal clues:** "I told you so...you should have known (or done) better... not again!...I'm only trying to help you...some day you'll thank me" **Body language**: Furrowed brow, pursed lips, a long sigh, pointing a finger, folded arms and tapping foot, hitting

SKILL BUILDER 35. Think of + and − Parent behaviors of your real-life parents and grand-parents. How many do you also have? Are they positive and appropriate? If not, work on replacing them with more appropriate behaviors to be a + Parent!

CHILD (+ and −)

Your internal *Child* is present from birth, probably before. Your feelings, good and bad, are in your *Child* and there's a positive and negative side.

Your **OK Kid (+ C),** also called the *Natural Child*, is fun-loving and indulgent, joyously happy, loud, energetic, creative, imaginative, sharing, and loving. **Verbal clues**: "Can I ... I wanna ... neat ... cool ... Wow! **Body language**: Giggles, touching, closeness, hugs, playful teasing.

Your *Not OK Kid* **(- C),** also called the *Adapted Child,* is guilty, fearful, depressed, jealous, sadistic or masochistic, or defiant. **Verbal clues**: "I can't/won't ... I'm afraid ... do I have to? ... sorry ... wups ... it's mine, gimme ... you're stupid ... I did it again." **Body language**: Quivering lip, downcast eyes, tears, withdrawn, whining/sulking, temper tantrums, acting out, vandalism.

SKILL BUILDER 36. How's your Child? More OK than not? Understand and accept Not OK Kid feelings and when they occur find ways to offset them with an OK

Kid mental hug ("you're still OK") or + Parent pat on the back. Hurt feelings are inevitable but should not be seen as a judgment of anyone's worth.

ADULT (A)

Your internal *Adult* is the manager, analyzer, data processor, coordinator, interpreter, mediator between your *Parent* and *Child*. Quite a family! Your *Adult* asks good questions and makes good decisions. Robert Louis Stevenson described how it functions: "I have these honest serving men. They serve me well and true. Their names are What and Where and How and Why and Who."

The *Adult* in you asks good questions. It begins to emerge at about age 1, when you begin to understand "me" from "not me," that a rattle or toy is not part of your body. Psychologically, it is when you become aware you are a separate individual (self-concept). **Verbal clues**: Verbal clues: "I hear you saying … I agree (or disagree) because … I wonder if … could it be? … being aware and attentive and asking good questions. **Body language**: Gestures and mannerisms that match the verbal clues.

SKILL BULDER 37. How active and effective is your Adult? Is it mediating well between your Parent and Child? If not, how can you improve its function and make your Parent, Adult, and Child a happier family?

SKILL BUILDER 38. Look for examples of + and − Parent, OK Kid, Not OK Kid, and Adult behaviors on the job and in your daily life. There are helpful tips in the next few pages.

SKILL BUILDER 39. If your Parent, Adult, and Child were circles, would they all be the same size? If not, what can you do to equalize them?

STROKES

Anything you say or do or is said or done to you is a *stroke*. There are three kinds:
1. **Warm fuzzies.** Genuine, kind, positive words or actions. Examples: Pat on the back, a real compliment or sincere thanks and any genuinely friendly gesture
2. **Cold pricklies.** Unkind or hostile words or actions. Examples: ridicule, ignoring someone, a "back-handed compliment" or demeaning comment.
3. **Plastic fuzzies.** Phony, insincere, artificial or "forced" social behavior. *Examples:* An unfeeling, empty "have a nice day" or "hello," a "frozen" or weak smile, a limp handshake.

SKILL BUILDER 40. Do you give enough warm fuzzies to others? Cold pricklies or plastic fuzzies? Try to ensure you give only warm fuzzies. They cost nothing and go a long way in building teamwork and high morale.

TRANSACTIONS and GAMES

A **transaction** is an exchange of strokes. Whenever you say or do something (a stroke) and another person responds (return stroke) there has been a transaction. A transaction is a **game** when it is a *win-lose* contest with a payoff. The payoff is a kick, usually to the loser's **Not OK Kid.**

Canadian psychiatrist Eric Berne originated this model. He named it **transactional analysis.** Using it, contacts between people can be shown graphically by two sets of circles of *Parent, Adult,* and *Child.* Lines drawn between them identify *strokes* given and received. Most *games* are a variation of a **"kick me"** transaction and at about a 4 mental age level -- really immature impulsive "kid stuff," a waste of time, and *always negative.*

When transaction lines cross there are hurt feelings or conflict, like bare electric wires touching, a psychological short circuit. Here are some game situations to avoid:

MINE'S BETTER'N YOURS

Someone tries to "one up" and "put down" another person, such as "my job's better'n yours" or "my company's better'n yours." The - *Parent* tries to kick the other person's *Not OK Kid,* or a *Not OK Kid* puts down an *OK Kid.* ANTIDOTE: Center or ground yourself in your *Adult* and *call the game* by conceding the bottom line: "Yes, indeed, your (whatever's involved) is very good and may be better than mine." Game over!

UPROAR

This one's a crossed transaction between a critical – *Parent* hooking into the other person's *Not OK Kid* (- *Child*) by constant criticism, belittling, or chronic complaints. If the kicked *Not OK Kid* switches to a -*Parent,* transactions become a battle between two negative forces. ANTIDOTE: Plug in your *Adult* who asks questions and offers alternatives, protecting your *Child* against hurt feelings and burnout.

MUSEUM, ARCHAEOLOGY

This is a more sophisticated version of *Uproar* when a *- Parent* uses a more detailed memory of past mistakes and problems and cites them continually to kick the other person's *Not OK Kid*. **ANTIDOTE**: Center yourself in your *Adult* to stop the memory list. Acknowledge the point, ask or offer alternatives, and remain centered in your *Adult*.

AIN'T IT AWFUL

This game *appears* to be a parallel transaction between two *+ Parents* to complain about something. As this continues they become more upset, a sign they're hooked. They are also likely to upset anyone listening. What is really happening is they are kicking each other's *Not OK Kid* *(- Child),* a continuing exchange of negative strokes and a depressing conversation. **ANTIDOTE**: Go to your *Adult* and *deliver the punch line*: "Yes, it's really awful." If the game continues *redeliver* the punch line: "As I said, it's awful!" Game over!

YES, BUT...

This *appears* to be an *Adult-to-Adult* game-free transaction but it really isn't. The game player confides s/he has a problem and needs your help. But every time you suggest a solution it's answered with: "Yes but ..." and a lame excuse why it won't work. What's really happening is the person with the problem is responding from the *Not OK Kid* and not from the *Adult*.

It's a **kick me game** ending when you give up in exasperation, usually with something like: "Well, I don't know what else to tell you." Then, the game player picks up all the marbles, proving the problem is more than you can handle, and wins the game. **ANTIDOTE**: Center in your *Adult* and after about two suggestions are rejected with: "I see it's a big problem and that's all I can do (or think of) to help."

NIGYSOB

NIGYSOB is an acronym for *Now I've got you, you SOB!*. It's a game also called *Sweetheart*, named for the payoff punch begins. It's a hard game of a grudge held until just the right moment for a powerful **kick me** payoff. The victim believes a previous exchange was settled but the gamer is waiting for the ideal time to attack. At the opportune time and situation the gamer springs the trap and delivers the big kick.

For example, assume the President of the United States needs to use a bathroom and his car just happens to be passing by your home. A Secret Service agent asks if the President can use your bathroom. Of course, you agree. Your significant other offers coffee which is graciously accepted. A week before, you bought an expensive rare carpet and the first day it was put down you tracked muddy feet over it. Nothing was said at the time and you consider yourself lucky to escape criticism.

Now, however, significant other asks the President if he likes the carpet. The reply is a compliment of its beauty. The significant other then points out that it's a rare and expensive carpet. The Chief Executive compliments both of you for your good taste. "What, Mr. President, would you think of a person who, knowing its cost, tracked muddy feet over it the first day it was put down?" The trap is set. The President replies: "Such a person would be stupid, careless, and with no appreciation for beauty or cost." Significant other stares into your eyes and asks: "Sweetheart, do you know anyone like that?" **Ouch!**

ANTIDOTE: Process it through your *Adult* which has sharp perception. As the instant you are aware of what might be coming, go for the bottom line and apologize, thus kicking *yourself* and disarming the game player. Game over.

SKILL BUILDER 41. What is the P-A-C interaction in sexual harassment? How much of the + and - Parent, Adult, and + and - Child of each person is involved? What should it be? Hints: (1) consensual sex is between two OK Kids, permitted by their Adults and Parent; (2) Adult-Adult would be: "May I?" answered with a "No, thanks."

INTIMACY and SCRIPTS

Intimacy is a game-free relationship between two *Adults*. It is an open, trusting, healthy parallel transaction considered to be the ideal relationship. Why? Because the *Adult* is the only part of you that is in touch with the + and − sides of your *Child* and your *Parent* and that can see the *Parent, Adult,* and *Child* in others. If you can remain "grounded" and "centered" in your *Adult* you will more quickly detect a game. Your *Adult* protects you and helps overcome negatives. Intimacy is *not* a game because it is a direct, open, equal exchange of positive strokes (*warm fuzzies*) between game-free *Adults*. Beautiful! That's what close lifelong friendships are. A way to establish a game-free relationship is to have a ***contract partner.*** You *contract* with another person for feedback about a behavior you want to change. It isn't a contract until the other person agrees and contracts with you for feedback about their specific need for improvement . Contracts save time. You can meet, mention "contract time," and be immediately on frequency for open, personal feedback. It also reinforces a trusting relationship between the two ***Adults.*** True intimacy!

Scripts are sets of expectations of self and others. They can be realistic or unrealistic, based on personal bias or preconceived notions. The scripted person's attitude and behavior is as if playing a role, taking a part in a play. *Example:* A high-ranking military officer may be scripted to expect he or she will be accorded the same status and deference in civilian life.

SKILL BUILDER 42. How can you be sure you don't play games or have a negative script? For your own personal and professional growth you should know how your Parent, Adult, and Child interact with others and help your Adult protect you from game players. Who would be a good contract partner for you? Why not contract with her or him?

COPING WITH PROBLEM PEOPLE
HIDDEN AGENDAS

In her book *Peoplemaking,* Virginia Satir described five hidden agendas in people and organizations. Four are negative and one is positive.

1. **Blaming** is finding fault, disagreeing and also being

disagreeable, because you feel no one else makes any sense. Getting work done and reaching decisions really don't matter because it'll all be wrong anyway.

2. **Placating** is "sweet talking," peace at any price, that If you're nice everyone will be nice to you and to each Other – and is more important than getting work done or reaching decisions.

3. **Irrelevant** is going off on tangents and avoiding getting to the point because there isn't enough detailed information. Data gathering is as important as deciding. The work can wait.

4. **Super-reasonable** is accepting everyone's opinion regardless of its value because everyone has a right to an opinion and there may be some great truth in what ever anyone says or does. Discussion is better than deciding.

5. **Congruent**, being "together," the ideal agenda, being reasonable, honest, positive, and open, using facts and common sense, communicating clearly, and helping others to be congruent.

SKILL BUILDER 43. Do you have any of these hidden agendas? How much of each? Are you congruent? How can you be sure? Can you see any tendencies you have toward any of the others? Check yourself out by consulting others you know who are congruent.

DETECTING PROBLEM PEOPLE

Regardless of your position and title, you will meet and work with people who are a problem for you. Though their behavior varies they share similar distinctive characteristics:
1. Their behaviors are recognizable by you and others
2. Their attitude and behaviors are predictable
3. They are always difficult
4. Their reactions are usually unreasonable or exaggerated
5. They have a negative effect on others

Coping with them is easier when you are aware of why and how they got to be problem people. Though their behavior varies they share one factor in common: *their behavior pays off for them.* It is usually a long-term or lifelong pattern from early childhood, reinforced in their everyday behavior. Because it is deeply rooted there is little or nothing you can do to change them. And, you don't have the time or the skill. Trying to change them will subject *you* to needless additional stress. It isn't worth it. You could even become a problem person yourself! Instead, learn to prevent their behavior from interfering with you and your work. Be positive. They give you the opportunity to develop coping skills and improve your leadership skills. And the greater their problem behavior, the more you can grow by effectively coping with it. Here they are:

1. **BULLDOZER.** Usually a male with "a short fuse," a bully or barking dog.
   Their strategy: Overpower, might makes right, nice

guys finish last. Over-reacting keeps everybody away at a safe distance. Bosses back down.
Their tactics: Shoot first, think later; blast, over-react, outshout others.
Effect on others: Fear, avoidance.
Recommended coping: Don't fight. You'll lose! Try a 1-2-3 takedown: "I hear you (1) but I wonder if … (2) … and what others think" and (3) sidestep their anger, let them bark (vent) within reason.

2. **BADMOUTH** are chronic complainers, critics, gripers, usually with an acid tongue.
   Their strategy: Finding fault is the best way to win and feel good about yourself and prove your self-worth.
   Their tactics: Always criticize, belittle, put down any one and anything.
   Effect on others: Disillusionment, avoidance, a major negative influence.
   Recommended coping: Be positive. Calmly, confidently continue. Don't get hooked emotionally.

3. **LOST SOUL,** clinging vine, wet blanket, drifting helplessly.
   Their strategy: The world is a dangerous place. I can't make it!
   Their tactics: Be helpless and there will always be someone to rescue you.
   Effect on others: Frustration, irritation, anger, and avoidance.
   Recommended coping: Don't be a rescuer! Continually rescuing them takes time and can lower standards, erode team spirit, and keep lost souls passive.

Encourage involvement. Reward them for finishing tasks and emphasize *they* did it, a personal achievement.

4. **SWEETHEART** is sickeningly sweet, super agreeable but superficial.
    Their strategy: Be nice and everyone will be nice to you. No need to do anything, just smile and be sweet and everyone will love you.
    Their tactics: Do little or nothing, keep smiling, and never criticize.
    Effect on others: Avoidance, distrust, impatience
    Recommended coping: Reward them for being critical. Reparenting them or being *their* sweetheart can make them more passive.

5. **SANDBAGGER** is a foot dragger, procrastinator, and passive obstructionist.
    Their strategy: Delay long enough and you win. Change is bad anyway. Anything new is dangerous: "If it ain't broke, don't fix it."
    Their tactics: Use every possible roadblock to avoid work and change.
    Effect on others: Avoidance. Their negativism is contagious.
    Recommended coping: Try to match every negative with a positive. Calmly state or repeat goals and what's needed. Be patient, steadfast. Keep cool. Seeing you sweat encourages them.

6. **EXPERT** really is an expert, knowledgeable, skilled, experienced, but tend to overthink and obsess and s/he

often lack common sense.
Their strategy: Knowledge is power. Not knowing is failure.
Their tactics: Consciously or unintentionally put down others.
Effect on others: Inferiority feeling, avoidance, lowered morale.
Recommended coping: Acknowledge, accept, and use their expertise but take the ball back with: "Yes, and it may also be that …".

7. **ODDBALL** is a loner with unusual thinking or behavior and usually socially isolated or withdrawn.
Their strategy: Don't grow up. Being a kid with childish fantasy or being different is safer and better.
Their tactics: They behave as if they are in a world to themselves, daydream, are easily distracted, and have difficulty following direction.
Effect on others: Avoidance
Recommended coping: Involve them. Help them keep focused.

8. **SECRET AGENT:** The most dangerous, usually above average intelligence but devious, deceptive, conspiring.
Their strategy: The sweetest victory is winning by clever manipulation and outsmarting authority figures they see as stupid and deserve to lose anyway.
Their tactics: Subtly outmaneuver, indirectly outwit everyone, especially authority figures. The end always justifies the means. Deceive and use others to help.

Effect on others: Avoidance, fear, and feeling used and dirty.

Recommended coping: Avoid 1-to-1 conversation. It can later be denied, distorted, or used to start a rumor. Keep contact public, witnessed. Be aware they often dupe or recruit others unaware of their real intent.

DO'S AND DON'TS

1. **DO** keep a safe, optimal distance from them but do not isolate yourself from them. Keep them in sight.
2. **DO** focus on work to be done, not personal differences.
3. **DO** shift into the scientific method of problem solving (Skill 4).
4. **DO** stay focused, centered, grounded. Do not get distracted.
5. **DO** take care of yourself! Don't get emotionally involved. That's how they win.
7. **DON'T** try to change them. You're not a therapist, don't have the time, and you're facing a lifelong entrenched pattern behavior.
8. **DON'T** fight them. That takes time and energy, raises your stress level, and you may well lose.
9. **DON'T** excuse them or ignore them. Neutralize their effect (damage control).
10. **DON'T** play games. They're better at it. If they involve you in a game, center yourself in your *Adult* and either call the game or decline to play.

FIVE NEVERS

1. **NEVER** put down or belittle anyone, except yourself which is always OK?

2. **NEVER** lecture or preach. It can sound condescending and like a – *Parent* to a *Not OK Kid.*
3. **NEVER** raise your voice or order people around. It looks like you're losing it.
4. **NEVER** threaten, ridicule, harass or probe needlessly. Focus on getting the work done.
5. **NEVER** lose control. Then everyone's lost. If you're getting upset, take a break.

SKILL BUILDER 44. Review the types of difficult people. Which really bugs you more than others? Study their strategies, tactics, and the best way to cope with them. Imagine the worst possible situation and mentally rehearse how you will handle it. By doing this you won't be caught off guard and you will cope much better.

COPING TACTICS

1. STAY COOL! Ground, center, stabilize yourself physically and mentally. If seated, sit upright, solidly balanced on the chair, both feet on the floor. Be aware of your breathing. Keep it regular. There's a tendency to breathe more rapidly when stressed and that can lead to more anxiety. A good way to take time to relax more and cope better is by first thanking them: "I want to thank you for sharing your (suggestion, thoughts, feelings). I appreciate that." As we were taught in childhood "please" and "thank you" are magic words. These verbal techniques can disarm, defuse, and cool.

2. APOLOGIZE even when you're right! That's more word magic. "I can see you're upset and I'm sorry about that," then acknowledge *your* feelings: "It's upsetting for me, too." Expressing regret does not mean conceding an-

anything. This does not weaken but actually strengthens your position, shows your openness, and can pay off if the matter goes to a higher level. Many lawsuits are by people who feel wronged and would not have sued if there had been a simple apology earlier.

3. STATE YOUR CASE calmly and clearly. Stick to facts not feelings. Try *reframing* the situation by referring to "it," not you or the problem person. Then, if conflict continues the conversation can be more objective, less personal. It is easier to negotiate or resolve a situation when both parties stick to facts and avoid personalities. Many problems are solved at this step.

4. MAKE AN OFFER. Try for a win-win exchange of gifts, what you consider a fair resolution. Try: "What can *we* do to correct it?" or "if you see a way to fairly solve this I'll gladly work with you on it." At this stage you can shift into the steps of the scientific method.

5. SIDESTEP CHARGING BULLS. Be a matador. Ignore irrelevant behavior. "Be kind to dumb animals." Some leaders overreact, overdo, and overkill. *Choose* not to be the victim. Insulate, isolate, ground and center yourself.

6.   DISARM, GRACIOUSLY. "I appreciate your input...I'm always willing to listen...sorry if what I said offended you...I hear what you're saying but..." Express your openness, then what's needed. It encourages others to do the same.

7. **COLUMBO TACTIC:** Adapt and lower yourself, put yourself down by playing dumb: "I get confused, let me see if I understand this correctly, if we___ then___. Is that right?" Often the other person provides loopholes not obvious before when the problem situation is repeated.

8. **HUMOR** can be an effective coolant and lubricant to overheated verbal engines but to do so it must be used wisely and well. It should never be used if there's any chance it can be misconstrued or to attack or hurt. To develop this skill watch TV comedies, read comic strips, and observe humorous situations in everyday life.

9. **VELVET GLOVE** or **SCREWDRIVER.** This is a soft sell indirect approach that usually begins with "I wonder if ___" or "could it be ___" or "if we ___ what would happen?"

10. **SANDWICHING** and **PAIRING.** *Sandwiching* is to begin and end a negative comment or a constructive criticism with a positive statement between, thus sandwiching in the negative. Example: "That was a fine job you did. You might also try to ... and I'm sure it'll turn out well." *Pairing* "softens the blow "of any negative comment or constructive criticism by matching it with a positive comment, still delivering a corrective message: "Your work is really top notch and I'm sure this was a minor glitch." This tactic may take a few moments more but pays off in higher morale and productivity.

11. **USE THE TEAM.** Sometimes many heads *are* better than one. Participative management empowers workers

helping them feel part of decision making and completing assignments. It raises morale and group consensus helps neutralize problem people.

12. REFER OUT OR UP. If a conflict situation causes continued misunderstanding of a policy or procedure it may be wise to refer it to a higher level for further information, consultative advice, a decision, or the clout of higher power. Be aware that doing this too often may weaken higher management's confidence in you. A variation is to reschedule action or discussion to a later date, delegate someone to gather more data, or appoint a committee to do so.

13. DO NOTHING. Laotse in ancient China knew about confused situations. He compared them to muddy water. Left alone, undisturbed, it usually clears by itself. Some conflict situations fade over time. It's true "mighty oaks from tiny acorns grow" and it may be wiser to resolve conflicts when they are small and prevent them from getting worse. It's a judgment call and test of leadership skill.

TALK TACTICS

How many ways can you interact with another person? Here are 14:

1. SILENCE is one of the most effective and *least used* verbal tactics. It is the *strategic* use of pauses, pacing, time, and timing. Common *misuse* is to wait too long to say something or, conversely, to speak too quickly or interrupt a "heavy" conversation breaking the mood.

2. **SUPPORT** is given to reassure, sympathize with, or encourage. It can be done verbally or nonverbally with a nod, wink, pat, or gesture.

3. **SELF-DISCLOSURE** is sharing your own personal experiences in past or present similar situations. Use it wisely! Confessing too much weakness might lessen confidence in your leadership ability or competence.

4. **INDIRECT APPROACH.** This is the "velvet glove" approach of subtly leading the conversation by asking questions such as "What else could you/we do? ... I wonder if ... what would happen if ... or the *Columbo technique*: "I don't know, I'm not too sure, but maybe you could ,,,"

5. **DIRECT CONFRONTATION.** This can be *tough love* or a softer *telling it like it is*. Use when there is little time for discussion or a firm decision must be made but use it cautiously at other times because of possible negative effect.

6. **ASK QUESTIONS.** This is the "Socratic method" encourages more or deeper thought, reflection, reframing. Don't overdo it. That might seem badgering or belittling.

7. **HELP EXPLORE ALTERNATIVES** is best done *indirectly* or may sound like you're being domineering.

8. **CLARIFY.** Stop and review, rephrase, reframe the situation. This cools hot topics, allows more time to vent hurt feelings, go to better closure.

9. **HERE AND NOW FOCUS,** strictly limited to what's happening at the moment with no reference to the past.

10. **THERE AND THEN FOCUS,** digging deeper into the past for what's behind or beneath present problem.

11. **PHYSICAL FOCUS** on facial expression, posture, and mannerisms: "I can see you're upset and I want to do whatever I can to help…"

12. **VERBAL BEHAVIOR FOCUS** on what is said, and how (tone of voice, rate of speech, choice of words). "I hear you and I want to help…"

13. **FEELINGS FOCUS** on what you or the other person is feeling rather than the facts involved: "How do you feel about it?" A useful question! You may not agree with a person's feelings but allowing those feelings to be vented relieves tension, often for both of you.

14. **HUMOR** can be an effective icebreaker, to lessen distance, lower resistance and defenses, and cool hot tempers. Time, timing, and content are important. Never use it to ridicule or laugh at anyone, except yourself which is always OK. To be effective, humor must be natural and not forced or hostile.

SKILL BUILDER 45. On a separate sheet, make three columns: ME, MAYBE, and NOT ME. Go down the list of talk tactics and write under the ME column those you regularly use. Under the MAYBE column write those you sometimes use and those you haven't used under the NOT ME column. Think about the value of each. Why not use whichever is appropriate at the time?

COUNSELING SKILLS

You don't have to be a therapist to give advice. While it's better to help people find answers to their problems themselves, there comes a time in ever leader's work life when some kind of counseling is needed. Here are some helpful counseling skills:

EMPATHY

Empathy is *fellow feeling,* often described as "walking in someone else's shoes." It is to feel what another person feels as if you were that person. It differs from sympathy which is more understanding of someone's situation and not necessarily actual feelings. A sympathetic person might say: "I understand your situation." An empathic person would say: "I know how you feel" or "I've been there." Empathy goes beyond sympathetic understanding to a realization of "there but for the grace of God go I." Psychotherapist and teacher Carl Rogers considered empathy a key requirement of therapists, an *unconditional positive regard* for others.

Empathic listening is an important part of counseling and mentoring. Without it you are only a listener and can only understand what is said to you and not the *feeling tone* (the emotional part of the conversation). Empathic listening means to "see with a third eye" and "hear with a third ear." It is "to read between the lines" for underlying feelings. It involves *unconditional positive regard* for others, seeing them as members of the human race to be treated with the respect and dignity. There are many frustrations with policies and procedures as well as with people. *Empathic interaction* is the way to overcome negative feelings, enhance personal commitment (yours and others), and build teamwork.

REALIZE SKILL 2 !

The parting advice to help you realize **Skill 2** is from Edward Everett Hale:

>To look up and not down,
>To look forward and not back,
>To look out and not in,
>And to lend a hand.

FOR FURTHER STUDY

Listening skills and interacting

Allport, G.W., & Postman, L. *The psychology of rumor.* New York: Holt, Rinehart, and Winston, 1947.

Boje, D.M. *Johari window: The psychodynamics of leadership and influence.*

Festerheim, H., & Baer, J. *Don't say yes when you want to say no.* New York: McKay, 1975.

MacHovec, F.J. *Games we all play and shouldn't.* White Plains NY: Peter Pauper Press, 1974.

Satir, V. *Peoplemaking.* Palo Alto CA: Science and Behavior Books, 1972.

Stewart, I., & Joines, V. *TA today: A new introduction to transactional analysis.* Chapel Hill NC: Lifespace.

Tannen, D. *That's not what I meant.* New York: Ballantine, 1986.

Tannen, D. *You just don't understand.* New York: Ballantine, 1990.

Body language

Ekman, P. *Telling lies: Deceit in the marketplace, politics, and marriage.* New York: W. W. Norton, 2001.

MacHovec, F.J. *Body talk: A handbook of nonverbal behavior.* White Plains NY: Peter Pauper Press, 1975.

SKILL 3

MOTIVATE AND MENTOR!
You as coach and team builder

This third skill of leadership skills is on team building and using the group process. Effectively leading a team or group is more like being a coach than a direct supervisor. To coach a winning team requires a working knowledge of group dynamics, how people work individually and together in a dynamic whole. If there is a secret to team building it is the skill to lead a group toward a goal without being overbearing or leading by fear, threat, or force. The Chinese philosopher LaoTse wrote: "When the best leader's work is done the people proudly proclaim 'look what we accomplished together.'" He also wrote: "To lead, appear to follow." It's *participative management* but LaoTse knew it 2500 years ago in ancient China!

YOUR TEAM EXPERIENCE

If you ever feel your leadership experience is in any way limited, reflect on the leadership and followership you have had throughout your life in such areas as family, childhood, playmates, school, work, the military, recreational activities, individual or team sports, church or temple, clubs, and committees. Most people are pleasantly surprised to realize they have had leadership experience outside the workplace. The personal qualities of effective leadership outside the work setting are the same as those of quality leadership on the job.

SKILL BUILDER 46. *From the above and also in your life, what leadership roles have you had? Include work, sports, volunteer and youth programs. Bottom line: You are not as inexperienced as you may think.*

TEAM OR JUST A GROUP?

Groups are persons with similar interests or job responsibilities, with shared goals, or who pool their knowledge and skills. "The full orchestra surpasses any one instrument." The conductor doesn't play an instrument but lead and motivate others to do so and the best conductors get masterful performances from them. A team is more than just a group because its members work more closely together and more actively to achieve goals. There is more mutual trust, more fellow-family feeling, commitment, and clearer sense of mission and personal responsibility. Team members see their work as a making a difference, a contribution.

Lose a team member and work suffers. Lose group members and they can be replaced without significant loss. The secret of building teamwork and what transforms a group into a team is *mutual needs satisfaction.* Everyone gives something positive and gets something positive in return. Psychologists call it *psychic income.* It satisfies Maslow's higher need levels of *self-esteem* and *self-actualization.* **Skill 1** focused on who you are and ways to develop more self-awareness. Understanding individual differences in others flows naturally from understanding yourself. This in turn leads to accepting differences and making good use of them to build a high functioning team. But if everyone is a "rugged individualist" is it possible to develop a close-knit team that functions as the proverbial "well oiled machine"? Not only is it possible, it is the key to success of leading corporations and nations.

Workers and citizens bring to a company and to government the strengths of their personalities as well as their abilities and skills. Group and team participation can be *an exchange of gifts*. Mutual collaboration forges the links in the chain that makes groups and teams stronger than any of its individual members. The whole becomes greater than the sum of the parts: *synergy*. Superb teamwork is synergistic but won't happen unless and until the team "gels" into a dynamic whole, unity in diversity, when individual differences enrich and never interfere with the work at hand.

SKILL BUILDER 47. Use the above material to critique our work unit and your role as team leader or team member. Is the work unit more a group than a team? What percentage of each? Why? Think about individual differences in education, training, and experience. How do they enrich and strengthen the whole? Does familyand fellow feeling overcome any personal or personality differences? How can it be strengthened?

GROUP POWER

Leaders have shaped history. While it is debatable whether leaders shape times or times shape leaders, it is a fact that there is power in leaders and leadership. Examples are Alexander the Great, Julius Caesar, and Genghis Khan who conquered many lands, Lord Nelson who made naval history, and Washington's leadership in war and peace and who shaped a nation. Moses, Buddha, Jesus, and Muhammad founded religions that have endured for more than a thousand years.

It is also true that groups have power. There can be no leader without loyal followers and when followers join together and organize, they too shape history. There would be no religions, victorious armies, or lasting governments without the support of people in them. Their power is reflected in shared worship services, voting, and heroic service in war-time. A secret of team leadership is knowing and productively using the group process.

If a leader is a tool, the team is a machine. A well functioning team is society in miniature and a family unit. Like all families, there are different personalities that may - sometimes clash. But there is a positive strength that overcomes all differences: the additive effect of team member skills and strengths. The best teams succeed by harmonizing the positives and ignoring the negatives. It is an exchange of gifts. The bottom line in teamwork is the reality that more heads are better than any one of them.

Ways to use group process:

    1. Relying on the group and using it when possible and practicable rather than taking the lead directly.

    2. Realizing you don't *own* the group or anyone in it. Like team members they *share* in the experience of the group.

    3. Realizing you may not have all the answers and using participative management in *an exchange of gifts* of leader and team member skills.

    4. Emphasizing positives and neutralizing negatives by reinterpreting and reframing negatives in a more positive light.

5. Making every day *psychic income payday* by giving compliments, sharing good feelings, and recognizing tasks well done and special effort.

6. Believing and practicing the *Golden Rule* by treating others as you would want to be treated.

Brainstorming is another way of discovering team member skills and knowledge as well as problem solving. It can be used by first posting or announcing ground rules to ensure a free flow of ideas and suggestions. One rule is that anything goes, even the most out-of-the-box seemingly ridiculous ideas. Another rule is everyone has a right to peak and be heard in a free give-and-take without criticism. It is helpful to post the ideas on a wall with poster paper and masking tape. When ideas cease flowing, the team by consensus reviews the ideas. The object is to revise, combine, or generate new ideas. Often a new way of solving the problem emerges of and by itself, the acid test of group power.

SKILL BUILDER 48. Have you used any of these team building ways to harness group power? If not, why not? How can you improve your team leader skills? Promise yourself to use them.

WINNING TEAMS

1. Team members *identify* with the organization and its ideals. Really effective teams have members that feel the team is as much a part of them as they are parts of the team.
2. Team members feel *empowered*, that they have a voice in what's happening. The team leader is seen more as a

sharing partner than an authority figure. They feel free to differ with the team leader and have no antagonism toward the leader. Differences are resolved by *sharing* insights and alternatives, not by the leader's decision.
3. Team members *learn* from and *share* with each other their skills, strengths, and expectations. They are open, accepting, cooperative, and readily volunteer for whatever is needed. There is a strong and positive *group personality*.
4. The team *adapts* well to change and functions well under pressure.

LOSING TEAMS

1. Team members are *overly dependent* on the leader, rarely volunteer, and have a narrow focus (tunnel vision).
2. There is *poor communication* up, down, and between members.
3. There is *low morale, indifference,* and *apathy.*
4. The team makes *frequent errors, poor decisions,* and there is *more waste.*

SKILL BUILDER 49. *How does your team rate according to the signs of healthy and unhealthy teams? What are its strengths? Weaknesses?*

IDEAL TEAM MEMBERS

What traits are typical of the ideal team member? A study of 150 executives of Fortune 500 companies yielded four traits of whom they considered the best team players. They reported that the best team members: *avoid office politics, support their supervisors, and meet deadlines and responsibilities*

SKILL BUILDER 50. How would you rate yourself as a team member according to the Fortune 500 study? How would you rate your team members? How do your traits and theirs compare? Same, better, or worse? What does this tell you about your team leadership?

MENTORING

A **mentor** is a wise and trusted adviser, counselor, or teacher. The word comes from Greek mythology. Mentor was an elderly friend and counselor to Odysseus and his son Telemachus. Mentoring is more than teaching. It is advice and counsel enriched by wisdom and insight, experience and skill not in books or manuals. Mentoring is a sacred trust, a special relationship between two people joined together by a common interest toward a common goal, one that mentor and mentee may never forget. Words used to describe it include being a "Dutch uncle, big brother or big sister, contract partner."

Your best friends are mentors. So were your grandparents, aunts, and uncles. *Alcoholics Anonymous* sponsors are mentors. In amateur or ham radio they're called "Elmers." In the army they're *old hands* and *old salts* in the navy. Mentors in history and the theater:

Leaders: Julius Caesar to Mark Anthony; Lawrence of Arabia to Arab tribal leaders; Gandhi to Hindus, Muslims, and the British.

Teachers: Socrates to Plato, Plato to Aristotle, Aristotle to Alexander the Great

In movies: *Wizard of Oz* (Dorothy to the scarecrow, tin man, and lion); *Camelot* (Merlin to King Arthur); *My Fair Lady* (Rex Harrison to Audrey Hepburn); *Phantom of the Opera* (the phantom to the singer); *Star Wars* (Obewankenobe to Luke Skywalker); *The King and I* (Deborah Kerr or Jody Foster in the more recent version); *Arthur* (John Gielgud to Dudley Moore).

THE BEST MENTORING

Mentors help those mentored (*mentees*) to self-actualize. Signs of the best mentoring:
1. Focused attention, absorption, concentration. They are more "with it."
2. Little or no anxiety, fear, or defensiveness. They are more relaxed, spontaneous, and expressive.
3. Increased trust, self-confidence, and courage shown in increased initiative and appropriate risk taking.
4. Positive, accepting attitude, more receptive to new ideas. They welcome and help facilitate change.

Effective mentoring generates enthusiasm and energy that results in higher quality and productivity in the workplace and self-actualization in workers. Mentors are wise and trusted. Wisdom comes from years of experience and trust is earned, not learned. By sharing wisdom, insight, judgment, and experience, mentors do more than teach. Some tips to master *your* mentoring!
1. ***Know your subject or skill area.*** There is no substitute for mastery.
2. ***Accept everyone you mentor*** as unique individuals who learn at their own pace and in their own way.

3. *Build family and fellow feeling* between you, more brother or sister than parent-child.
4. *Help them recognize abilities and potentials* not yet realized and facilitate developing and applying them well. As Shakespeare put it: "Since you cannot see yourself so well as by reflection I, your glass (mirror) will modestly discover you to yourself, that of yourself you as yet know not" (*Julius Caesar*, Act 1, Scene 2).
5. *Help them experience the satisfaction of mastery beyond learning*, in a skill earned and developed, tasks done well. Share their joy.
6. *Criticize constructively* and when discussing anything negative, add and finish on a positive note.
7. *Give to get*. Out into practice the advice in the old adage "it is better to give than to receive" which Shakespeare wrote "is twice blessed. It blesses the giver and the receiver."
8. *Practice what you preach!* Be a role model who motivates and inspires others, seeing yourself and your work as making a difference, leaving the world (your job and company) better than you found it. When those you mentor do the same they, the company, and the world *will be better*!

SKILL BUILDER 51. *Are you mentoring anyone? Do you have a mentor yourself? If you are mentoring, review this material from time to time to do it well. If you have no mentor think of someone you'd like to mentor you. Why not discuss it with her or him?*

THE MANAGERIAL GRID

This is a useful way to explore how far your leadership style is task-oriented or people-centered. In their book *The managerial grid,* Blake and Mouton constructed a 9-point graph on two axes: people vs. task:

```
       9
P      8
E      7
O      6
P      5
L      4
E      3
       2
       1  2  3  4  5  6  7  8  9
              T A S K
```

Looking at extremes, Blake and Mouton call a 9-task 1-people position ***authoritarian***, a leadership style that insists on following schedules and meeting deadlines, direct orders, strict controls, and more criticism than support that stifles creativity and discourages collaboration. The opposite extreme, a 1-task 9-people position is called ***country club***, leaders who so value relationships they trust workers to get the job done without supervision but with lots of encouragement.

The 1-1 leader is ***impoverished***, passive and permissive, an absentee boss detached and indifferent, uncommitted to task and uncaring in relationships. A 5-5 leader is in the mid-range, task-oriented and people-centered. But this is not the recommended position. A 9-9 position is the ***team*** *leader* who attends to task but also to people, with strengths in both areas.

SKILL BUILDER 52. *Where do you place yourself on the Managerial Grid? Why? Is this best for you or the organization? Both? Ask others if they agree with your choice. Use this to better understand your leadership and management style.*

TRANSFORMATIONAL LEADERSHIP

There are fads and favorites in leadership theory that peak and fade just as in other areas. *Transformational leadership* is a current trend. It's a leadership style that *empowers* workers to grow personally and feel they and their work makes a difference. George MacGregor Burns is a prime mover and major supporter of this model. In his 1978 book *Leadership* he stressed the importance of leaders having and applying high moral values. Doing so changes leadership from transactional to transformational in its effect.

Burns sees leadership is *transactional* when work is completed by bargaining such as offering a bonus, chance for promotion, or other reward. This is at a lower level than *transformational* leadership that focuses on a worker's personal growth as well as job satisfaction. Referring back to the personality theories in *Skill 1*, transactional leadership is behaviorist since it uses reward and reinforcement. Transformational leadership is humanistic because it enhances self-esteem and facilitates self-actualization. Don't confuse Burns' transactional leadership with the Parent-Adult-Child transacting in *Skill 2*. They're not the same.

Burns calls the transformational role "the opposite of brute force" because it is based on satisfying mutual needs of leader and follower. He concedes leaders have "a spur of ambition" that drives them on but they can still have and practice "moral values." Most dictators throughout history have been amoral leaders because their ends justified any means. Often this resulted in a ruthless disregard for people and their needs. The "crucial variable" is the transformational leader's sense of mission and purpose and commitment to collective well-being that go beyond transaction. Still, Burns accepts and recommends transactional methods when appropriate.

Transformational leaders function as charismatic visionaries who connect with others on both thinking and feeling levels. They have a good sense of self (*Skill 1*) and are socially sensitive (*Skill 2*). Knowing themselves and others, they are uniquely prepared to motivate and inspire. They lead by example, delegate easily, and encourage participation. As with other theories and models, there is a down side. It is possible to become too emotionally involved. Carl Rogers, a humanistic psychologist, recommended what he called "provincial empathy," to feel for others but able to keep an optimal distance.

How transformational are you able and ready to become? The key is to blend personal strengths with the most appropriate type and use of power yet still help satisfy workers' needs and potential. A typical model for transformation follows these steps:

1. ***Create a vision*** consistent with core values and goals of the organization and also what's right.
2. ***Have a strategy*** to fulfill the vision (a map).

3. *Do it* (the journey). Communicate your vision, simply, positively, with impact.
4. *Lead by example* (walk the talk). *Be* the vision.
5. *Trust* employees and supervisors to succeed. Show it!
6. *Celebrate* by recognizing and rewarding every successful step along the way.
7. *Continually emphasize goals and values.*

SKILL BUILDER 53. How much of a transformational leader are you? It will be more helpful for you to ask others for feedback. How can you become more transformational?

FACETS OF TEAM LEADERSHIP
Team leaders fulfill have many roles:
1. *Interpreter* of information new and old
2. *Guide* through change (*change agent*)
3. *Facilitator* and *moderator* of group process
4. *Coach* bringing out the best in team members
5. *Mediator* of differences
6. *Catalyst* for group achievement
7. *Model* for others who aspire to leadership positions

THE IDEAL TEAM LEADER
The best team leaders have a clear sense of mission and goals and how best to achieve them. They lead by example and are good role models for others. They encourage and reward active involvement in the work at hand and help bring out the best in others. They *empower* others by welcoming input of ideas and suggestions before deciding alone (*participative management, transformational leadership*).

They build trust by trusting and build a team for the long term, not just for any single task.

They lead for the joy and satisfaction of work well done and not to build a personality cult. They accept differences as *opportunities* to share strengths. They see diversity as *enrichment* and not a weakness. And they see problems as *opportunities* for personal and professional growth by sharing skills and ideas. Studies consistently show that effective leaders have these traits:

1. *Good communicators* (clear and concise)
2. *Good listeners,* accepting, patient and supportive
3. *Accommodating* (flexible and helpful)
4. *Enthusiastic* and *optimistic*
5. *Open, honest,* and *fair*
6. *Adapt well* to change and *help others* adapt

SKILL BUILDER 54. *Rate yourself on each of the team leader roles and traits. Think of an example of each from your work and experience. Improve your team leadership skills by reviewing these roles and traits from time to time and observing and consulting with other team leaders.*

Flying airliners is an awesome responsibility. Besides flying the planes, pilots are team leaders for the crew. Studies show pilots with fewest errors, property damage, and accidents were warm and friendly, self-confident, and handled stress well. The same research found those with significant errors, property damage, and accidents tened to be arrogant and dictatorial, boastful and egotistical, and passive-aggressive.

SKILL BUILDER 55. How do you compare in the traits of successful airline pilot team leaders? Do you have any of the negative traits listed? How can you be sure? How can you find out?

TEAM LEADER STYLE

In ancient Rome, Terence wrote: "Do all things in moderation." 500 years before, Buddha described his philosophy as "the middle way." There are sayings like "the truth is usually somewhere in between" or "the truth is in shades of gray." Few differences are "worlds apart." People are really more similar than dissimilar. Differences and problems can often be resolved proceeding between the two poles of win and lose, in moderation, a middle path between overdoing and underdoing, neither too strict nor too permissive.

SKILL BUILDER 56. Being able to see strict, permissive, and moderate approaches to situations is a good skill building exercise. It helps you to more quickly grasp a situation, see it in total perspective, consider alternative solutions, and more easily do just the right thing at the right time. Think of a strict, permissive, and middle way of processing each of these scenarios:
1. *Reviewing and revising position descriptions.*
2. *Deciding on whether to have flex time.*
3. *Deciding company policy for office parties.*
4. *Setting a price on a product (supply-demand curve).*

DISSATISFIERS and SATISFIERS

In his book *Work and the nature of man*, Herzberg explained how the personalities and behaviors of leaders and managers can have positive and negative effects on productivity and the workplace. He chose the words *satisfiers* and *dissatisfiers* to describe them. **Dissatisfiers** have poor interpersonal relations, are poor supervisors, do not follow policy and/or procedures, focus on minutia, and tend to have personal problems. **Satisfiers** recognize and reward achievement, give workers psychic income, do quality work, and achieve advancement and help others do so.

SKILL BUILDER 57. Check yourself out. How much of a dissatisfier are you? How much a satisfier? How can you eliminate and prevent dissatisfier behavior and increase satisfier performance? It helps to think of dissatisfiers you have seen or heard about. Could they have been transformed into satisfiers? How?

TIME AND TIMING

Time is a precious commodity. When to introduce a subject, how best to speed or slow discussion, and when to take action and reach a decision is a vital leadership skill. Managing time and timing can make the difference between success and failure. There's much wisdom in the old saying: "Strike while the iron is hot." Shakespeare put it well: "There is a tide in the affairs of men which, taken at the flood, leads on to fortune" (*Julius Caesar*, IV, 3).

TIME SENSE AND NONSENSE

You've heard of common sense but what about time sense? *Time sense* is the skill to do the right thing at the right time in the right way. As a leadership skill there is a time to speak and a time to be quiet and let others speak, a time to intervene to control or allow more discussion. It's a skill that can be learned. There's a Zen proverb: "When the apple is ripe it drops from the tree by its own weight." To learn more about time and timing observe actors and actresses in movies and on TV, when and how they speak and use pauses. Some tips:

1. *Prioritize.* It's better to list important or sensitive agenda items earlier than later so there is enough time to process them and while you and others are fresh and more ready. Urgency and importance should be considered. Routine matters are best left last or earlier if they can be quickly completed.

2. *Work smart, not just hard.* For example, a task can be broken down into smaller parts (*chunking*). This can be done on paper, outlining or underlining key points. *Delegating* others to bring the pieces together or you can appoint a committee to do so. Avoid doing everything yourself. You may not have enough time and it may add to your stress level. Note date and time on all notes, reports, and letters. It takes only seconds and increases efficiency. Develop your own filing system for quick access. Try color coding folders. Find the best time to get things done, such as earlier or later in the day and when there are fewer interruptions. Buy and use the best technology (computers, software) most useful to you. Shop. You may not need all the "bells and whistles."

3. *Maintain control.* The secret is to manage time with a delicate touch, carefully and reasonably. End discussion too soon and you run the risk of being seen as heavy-handed and arbitrary. Let it ramble on and you risk being seen as weak and indecisive. There's an old saying that "we can't control events but we can control what we *do* with them." Running a business, an office, or a meeting is much like music. There is a beat to it, a rhythm and speed, even loud and soft parts.

Effective leaders are like orchestra conductors, closely observing and listening intently to the "music of meaning." They speed or slow the movement by strategic interventions. Done well this saves time. Done poorly time and energy are wasted. Know when to allow more time and when to set a time limit for discussion. Before deciding try asking: "Do we need more time to discuss this?" Know when it's wise to talk and when to listen, how to smoothly stop discussion to clarify, explain, or allow others to do so. Try apologizing: "I'm sorry but time's running out and we have to move on" or "It may be me, but I'd like to hear more about ___."

4. **KISS** *it*! (**K**eep **I**t **S**imple, **S**weetheart!), verbally and in writing. Scientists call it "Occam's razor," the simplest solution, approach, or explanation of more complicated alternatives. Usually the solution with the
fewest assumptions works well.

SKILL BUILDER 58. How many of these ways do you use regularly to manage and effectively use time? Do you choose which to use and when it is most appropriate? Which do you prefer? Why? Which do you avoid or never use? Why?

MANAGING MEETINGS

Three criticisms of meetings most often heard are: There are too many, too long, and too boring. Find ways to decrease the number of meetings, make them more useful, and more interesting. Some suggestions:

1. *Notify far enough ahead.* People tend to forget if notified too far in advance and there is usually less attendance if notified with too little time.
2. *Set a time limit.* If more time is needed, postpone or schedule another meeting. Consider delegating to someone or appointing a committee to investigate and report at the next meeting. This reduces discussion time during meetings.
3. *Keep the agenda simple.* Try for one page, one side, and uncluttered. Attach any needed information. Don't include it in the agenda.
4. *Stick to the agenda.* Don't stray. If other subjects or problems surface, add them to the next agenda, delegate or appoint a committee to handle them.
5. *Maintain control.* Allow and encourage discussion but set reasonable limits. Stifle windbags graciously.
6. *Thank everyone* as you adjourn for their attendance, attention, and their participation. It helps motivate and builds teamwork.

Why have meetings? That's really a good question. Meetings should be held at a minimum and only when necessary. Weigh the alternatives: phone calls, e-mail, 1-to-1 conversations, delegating to a committee, memos, and gathering data elsewhere. Meetings can be an inconvenience unless really needed and worthwhile. On the plus side, meetings involve workers in routine and special operations and add to their feeling a part of operations.

Meetings are appropriate when there is a need to impart information, implement plans, process business, solve a problem, reach a decision, or satisfy a mandatory requirement. One successful CEO commented half the meetings he attended throughout his career were unnecessary and agenda items handled without meetings. Another CEO felt all meetings he attended could have ended in half the time.

SCHEDULES AND AGENDAS

When you schedule a meeting, ensure the date and time does not conflict with other meetings or operations and is at a convenient time and location. Double check that the notices go out with enough lead time. Don't list involved or controversial subjects last. There won't be enough time to process them and by that time everyone (including you) will likely be eager to end the meeting. A suggested agenda:
1. Meeting title, subject, and who called the meeting.
2. Date, start and end time, place, directions if needed.
3. Purpose and desired outcome or alternatives.
4. Ground rules, if any.
5. Agenda items in priority order, with person(s) responsible for them.

CHAIRING AND SHARING

Many leaders run meetings poorly. How to keep you *off* that list:
1. *Start and end on time.* Mention the time schedule at the beginning and during the meeting to stay on time.
2. *Minutes.* Delegate someone to take notes if there is no secretary.
3. *Use a checklist agenda.* It's best when everyone has it. Refer to it as needed to prevent going off on tangents.
4. *Maintain control and focus.* Prevent monopolization and tangents. Limit discussion gracefully, be supportive and accepting even when stressed, encourage and reward participation, and protect the right to be heard.
5. *Be a good psychic paymaster!* See that everyone gets a "psychic income paycheck." It takes a bit more time but pays off in higher morale and better teamwork.
6. *Seek the simplest and best solution* decided by the fewest people who need to be involved.

PARLIAMENTARY PROCEDURE

Rules of order and *parliamentary procedure* are the methods used to transact business at formal meetings, so you should be familiar with them. The principles and practices are helpful even when not required at meetings. *Robert's Rules of Order* is the standard reference for many organizations as their standing rules and the conduct of meetings. The major leadership role is the ***presiding officer***. According to parliamentary procedure, presiding officers are expected to be:
1. Fair and impartial
2. Protect every member's right to be heard
3. Maintain order and focus on the business at hand

4. Draft and follow an agenda to meet unit needs
5. Ensure there is a quorum (1/3 of active members)
6. Ensure that decisions follow adequate discussion
7. Ensure compliance with by-laws, standing rules, and official policy
8. Entertain motions for the transaction of agenda business
9. Ensure minutes of the meeting are kept

Avoid commenting on motions on the floor other than to process them. Some may interpret your remarks as anopinion on what should be decided or it could incite a protest movement. If you are presiding and want to share your personal opinion on an agenda subject you can temporarily delegate the chair to another officer, state your opinion, then resume the presiding role. Presiding officers have the right to vote but usually do so to break a tie. In some cases it may be wise to create a tie to defeat the motion.

A *motion* is a proposal of action to settle a matter, usually an agenda item. It requires a second. Without a second the motion dies and cannot be discussed further. When seconded the presiding officer restates it to ensure everyone has heard it then asks: "Is there any discussion?"
At this time everyone is free to discuss it. Discussion ends when the presiding officer feels there has been enough discussion saying: "Are you ready for the question?" or a member "moves to close debate and vote on the question." If that member's motion is seconded it cannot be debated and requires a 2/3 vote to pass.

Motions that need a second: to adjourn, recess, table, take from table, postpone, limit/extend debate, refer to committee, previous question, amend, appeal the chair's decision, reconsider a vote, rescind (repeal), suspend rules, close or reopen nominations.

Motions that do <u>not</u> need a second and *not debatable,* decided by the chair: point of order, parliamentary inquiry, question a quorum, information request, and to withdraw a motion or a second.

It can get confusing when there are seconded motions and followed by other seconded motions. Keep track of them and dispose of them one at a time from the most recent to the original. It's like piloting a boat back to the home dock. The original motion is the home dock and the others are like moving from river to bay to ocean. Proper procedure is to move from the last motion (ocean) back to the nest to last motion (bay), to the original motion (river).

SKILL BUILDER 59. Do you know and do you apply these rules when you chair formal meetings? Do you manage informal meetings without parliamentary procedure well? How can you improve managing both formal and informal kinds of meetings?

NEUTRALIZE NEGATIVES

Some negativism is normal. Being corrected and correcting others are not usually pleasant experiences. Some people feel negative being told what to do by an authority figure. When orders come from a distant authority far removed from the workplace usually leave a more negative impression than receiving them first hand and face-to-face. Some resist change because they felt more secure comfortable before the change. It *is* peaceful when everything's predictable and routine. Work continues with the proverbial "dull roar," and we do tend to be creatures of habit. Some negativism is normal and unavoidable. From time to time someone will disagree with you or company policies or procedures. Honest differences of opinion may seem negative but when shared openly they do no harm. They're signs of a healthy work environment.

Negativism is destructive when it lowers morale and productivity. Chronically angry or frustrated workers feed the rumor mill or withdraw into sullen silence. On the other hand, everyone has an occasional bad day and when that happens negative reactions are to be expected. If something has really gone wrong it's healthy and normal to vent it. Unvented frustration can accumulate and is a real burnout factor. Chronic "bitching" can get to you, especially if it's from someone you dislike. Regardless of its negative impact, it makes good sense to realize there are *gripers' rights*. Everyone has the right to be:

> ... *wrong*
> ... *heard, and*
> ... *treated with respect*

Continuing uncontrolled negativism drains energy and enthusiasm, lowers morale and productivity, and leads to absenteeism and turnover. It creeps in like fog, often in little things, not necessarily a major conflict or event. When communication from a leader is 1-way, workers tend to passively submit but with a slow burn of irritation. "Apple polishing" is a negative interaction that irritates most leaders and engenders resentment in other workers. When negative factors are not corrected factions and cliques form and rumors flow. Criticism and blaming increase. It's a destructive downward spiral.

SKILL BUILDER 60. How good are you at managing gripers? Coping with negativism? Plan now how best to keep your cool under fire. Waiting until negativism is running out of control can put you and others at a disadvantage and it may be too late to neutralize it. Try mental rehearsal imagining the worst case scenario and how to handle it. You can't then be caught off guard. Chances are it won't be as bad as you imagined.

MANAGING DIVERSITY

Managing diversity is not only fair but it creates a positive work setting that values workers, appreciates differences, and ensures equal opportunity for everyone to reach their full potential. When openly accepted diversity in age, gender, and ethnicity enrich the work setting. Then there is more personal growth, empathy, mutual support and teamwork in what becomes family feeling and an exchange of gifts. This in turn increases openness and improves group problem solving. What emerges is a distinctive group or team identity with a "can do" spirit and high morale that can meet and surpass organizational and team goals.

Diversity is more than affirmative action which is a legally based goal to provide equal opportunity or to compensate for past discrimination. On the other hand, diversity is ethically based acceptance and valuing of differences and the uniqueness of every individual. *Diversity management* is strategically created and maintained positive environment where differences are understood, accepted, valued, and enables workers to reach their full potential. Gardenswartz and Roew (1993) described the differences:

Affirmative action	**Diversity**
legal, quantitative	behavioral, qualitative
equal opportunity	appreciate differences
develop policies	develop people
protect rights, remedy wrongs	respect dignity
assimilates everyone	appreciates differences
opens doors	opens minds
Possible resistance:	*Possible resistance:*
denying the need	fear of change, loss
fear of losing power	reverse discrimination

If management is getting things done, then diversity management is ensuring they get done by a team that shares fellowship and trust, "unity in diversity." Team members work closely together as a unified whole though yet understand, accept, and appreciate their differences in age, gender, ethnicity, and personality.

SKILL BUILDER 61: *In the work group, compare each person's answers to these questions:*
1. *Favorite color?*
2. *Favorite food?*
3. *Favorite dessert?*
4. *Favorite car?*
5. *Favorite house style?*
6. *Favorite vacation place?*

Compare lists. It is unlikely any two will be identical. Yet, until these questions were asked it is likely you have worked together unaware of them. Discuss how what draws us together is stronger than our differences.

This *Skill Builder* showed how we differ in our choice of favorites things. There are many kinds of differences. Each presents an opportunity to learn about others, grow personally, and move an organization and society itself onward and upward.

Personality differences. No two people are alike. They differ in likes and dislikes, attitude and behavior. Even in close-knit teams there are individual differences in the personalities of team members. Everyone is a unique and distinctive person yet most can get along well and can work closely with others. Though similar interests make for close friendships and lasting marriages, there are some differences even between close friends and spouses. Most friends and spouses find these differences not only fascinating but in many cases what makes the other person especially attractive.

Gender differences. Studies have shown there are gender differences. While there are exceptions, men generally tend to be more individualistic and competitive. Women tend to be more social-relational. The differences involve nature (heredity) and nurture (environment). In the animal world males tend to be hunters and females gatherers and nesters. But there are more similarities than differences in the human species.

Religious differences. Religious freedom is a protected Constitutional right. It's unlikely you know the religious affiliation of all your neighbors and coworkers, yet these differences do not interfere with being a good neighbor or building teamwork.

Political differences. There can be heated arguments over political differences. Free speech guarantees an open hearing in local, state, and federal governments. But politics, even so-called *office politics*, can be divisive and lower morale and teamwork. Achieving work goals and building teamwork and morale should take precedence over politics.

Racial differences. Racism makes the news whenever there is violence or discrimination because of the color of a person's skin. Racial acceptance rarely makes news. Like differences between men and women, all minorities and the majority share far more similarities than differences.

Ethnic differences are more evident when immigrants arrive who speak a different language and have unique customs and traditions. But they are here by choice based on a wish to be American. As with the other differences listed here, there are shared values beyond differences.

SKILL BUILDER 62: Consider or discuss the following:
1. *It is possible to disagree without being disagreeable.*
2. *It is possible to achieve goals despite differences of opinion.*
3. *It is possible to find something positive even in the most negative situation.*
How can you or your group help make these statements a reality in the workplace?

BEYOND EMPATHY: VALUING OTHERS

Empathy is fellow feeling, putting yourself in another person's shoes, realizing what another person thinks and feels in a given situation. It is a vital part of diversity management. Unless you understand others you can't really work as closely with them. If you can't work closely with others you can't provide effective leadership. One way to show that you value others is by encouraging them to continue their personal and professional growth, on the job in routine tasks, taking on other tasks, classes and workshops, and added responsibilities.

SKILL BUILDER 63: Consider or discuss if there is a difference between empathy and encouragement? What ways can a job and the work place help a person grow? How can you and the team help others do so?

Title VII of the *Civil Rights Act* protects five ethnic differences from "disparate treatment" or "adverse impact:" those of *race, gender, religion, color*, and *national origin.* An effective way to prevent such incidents is to be sensitive to any possible negative effects from what you say or do. If you are present when someone says or does something that might demean the dignity or integrity of another it is wise to intervene immediately rather than wait discuss it later with the thoughtless person.

Waiting may lead the offended person to assume you and others agree with the demeaning comment or conduct. If it was unintentional and you over-react by intervening, little harm is done. It can be a reminder of the need to respect others and be responsible for what is said and done. If you are uncertain but uncomfortable about what is happening, you might comment: "I don't know if you were offended by this but I don't feel so good about what's just happened." It's important to quickly detect and as quickly neutralize negative behaviors. Otherwise, they can become a demoralizing influence that lowers morale and wrecks teamwork.

Synergy is a word for a work unit and team spirit that exceeds any person in the group. It starts with fellow feeling when sharing tasks and working toward team goals. It is an exchange of gifts. Fellowship grows into a family feeling of close mutual support. *Synergy* is when positive qualitative differences of team members blend together, their knowledge, skill, ability, enthusiasm, trust, energy, and radiate more power than any individual member or even the sum of all of them together. It is then the whole exceeds the sum of its parts.

There is a potential for synergy within individuals as well. Everyone brings to a work unit years of life experience, education and training, skills both learned and native or natural to that person. Positive ethnic differences and traits from other cultures can enhance teamwork, humanize and personalize it like a harmonious family. Shared similarities are far stronger than any differences. Similarities join rather than separate workers. An example of a strong shared value is the Golden Rule which has appeared throughout history, across time, language, and cultural differences.

The term "organizational culture" comes from research on the beliefs, values, customs, and languages of people around the world. Every culture has distinguishing features, a kind of personality of its own. The culture of an organization is formed from its mission and how things get done. "Rites of passage" are part of this culture, such as the education, training and experience to qualify for work in it. A vey important and fragile key factor is the quality of performance in addition to work skill. Here, motivation is a plus, enriched by the personality, interests, values, and fellow feeling of the individuals in the organization.

Changing of the guard in London, with its color and pageantry, reflects strong organizational identity. You can feel the energy in the bearing of the marchers, their attitude and behavior projecting confidence, commitment, and achievement. Every work unit has a distinctive personality. In science, when everything in an experiment goes well it is often described as *elegant.* Just as charisma distinguishes great leaders, elegance distinguishes the effect of work units in the quality and spirit of their Performance, its unique personality.

SKILL BUILDER 64: What's unique about your work unit? Describe its unique personality.

THE THREE V's

Three V's energize a work unit:

Values, shared and blended positively, from staff to the organization. Differences are *valued* as opportunities to share in an exchange of gifts between persons. This goes beyond understanding and acceptance and into shared values of openness, trust, and mutual support.

Vitality is to realize synergy from pooled energies, enthusiasm, and commitment, an active, doing, achieving team spirit.

Vision is to share ideas and ideals, goals and mission, at all levels. It is to see America in miniature in the work place, sharing in something that transcends and transforms differences into a strong bond of fellowship and an opportunity for personal self-actualization.

SKILL BUILDER 65: Think of and describe one thing you and your coworkers can do to help manage diversity better.

SKILL BUILDER 66: *Consider or if in a group discuss this poem by Etienne de Grellet (1771-1855). Do you agree or disagree with it? What are the pros and cons?*
  I expect to pass through this world but once;
  any good that I can do or any kindness I can show,
  let me do it now; let me not defer or neglect it,
  for I shall not pass this way again.

BIAS, HARASSMENT, AND DISCRIMINATION

Despite your best intentions there may still be some bias and harassment among your staff. Conscious effort is required to be aware of them and intervention should be prompt to prevent them from continuing and increasing. Bias, harassment, and discrimination have one thing in common: they are mean-spirited, unjustified, and always negative. No good comes of them. If you are present when anything negative and destructive happens, say or do something positive to stop it.

Philosopher Edmund Burke observed: "The only thing necessary for the triumph of evil is that good people do nothing." It is often better to apologize and be embarrassed for trying to correct what you thought was a negative situation than have an innocent person hurt without taking action. You never know how long the pain of being humiliated will last. It can "be the last straw" before legal action or resignation not only from the person hurt but others who witnessed it and became disillusioned.

Sexual harassment is not just inappropriate. It is unprofessional, inconsiderate, humiliating, and an attack on dignity and self-esteem. "Off color" remarks and dirty jokes border on sexual harassment and can have the same effect. Some women may smile or laugh but still feel uncomfortable or hurt. Sexual harassment can occur to anyone, man or woman, gay or straight. We live in a permissive society with gender and ethnic humor more freely used. The informality of a close-knit team increases the risk humor or personal relationships can become problems. A good rule is not to use humor or have a relationship you wouldn't want published in the newspaper or shown on TV news.

When confronting bias, discrimination, or sexual harassment use common sense and good judgment. Fair treatment and equal opportunity regardless of age, race, color, religion, national origin, or gender are *basic civil rights*. It's not wise to be a "watch dog" of "office Nazi" policing against bias and harassment. It's equally unwise to lightly dismiss incidents as "boys will be boys" or "girl talk." If you are open, honest, and considerate it will show. Anyone offended is more likely to feel free to discuss what happened and offenders more likely to discuss it and even admit their mistakes.

SKILL BUILDER 67. How would you handle these situations?
1. *You are on a break with a group of employees. A male worker tells increasingly explicit sexual jokes. One woman blushes but says nothing. Another just stares at the floor.*
2. *An older woman on your team nearing retirement confides that she thinks two young women in your office are lesbians.*
3. *You know that two of your team members not married to each other are having an affair.*

4. *You find a porno magazine on your secretary's desk. Would if the secretary was male or female, gay or lesbian? What if you discovered one of your staff is using the office computer to access a porno website?*

CHOOSE TO BE POSITIVE

Like opposite electrical charges, negativism can be offset by a positive charge. Being neutral has no effect on it and allows it to gain strength. Here are ways to generate positive energy and offset negativism:

1. *Self-disclosure,* sharing previous similar experiences you've had that ended positively.
2. *Offer positive alternatives.* This is more effective done indirectly such as by beginning with "I wonder if ___" or "what would happen if ___?"
3. *Be a spin master!* Put a "positive spin" by finding something positive about what's happening. The glass is *always half full,* never half empty.
4. *Sandwich or pair* positives with negatives as they arise. Make it a habit!
5. *Be a matador!* Gracefully sidestep any charging bulls. Consciously choose not to be anyone's target. Stay cool, factual, businesslike under fire, or it can become an ugly win-lose confrontation.
6. *Use "we" statements.* Begin with "we" or "it" instead of "I" or "you." That prevents blaming, such as *You* didn't…" **IT** is the problem, not *you* and not necessarily or entirely the worker. "We" encourages objectivity, doesn't hurt feelings, and enhances teamwork.
7. **Use an "I-then-so" sequence.** This helps clarify and analyze a problem situation and weaken any negatives.

"When (or whenever) ___, I (what does it do to you?) ___, and then (what happens) ___, so (end result)." This describes the problem and its effect. Sometimes leaders only troubleshoot a problem and try to ignore the effect on the leader. The "I-then-so" technique enables the worker to realize not only the problem situation but also he effect on the leader, the organization, and policy.

SKILL BUILDER 68. Put a "positive spin" on these comments made during a staff meeting:
1. *"That's the dumbest thing I ever heard"*
2. *"This office (or that department) can't do anything right"*
3. *"We've always done it this way. If it ain't broke, don't fix it."*
4. *"Well, the company's stock has dropped again."*
   Would your "spin" be any different 1-to-1 to the person speaking rather than at a staff meeting? Why?

WORKPLACE VIOLENCE

It is not unusual to see reports of troubled employees who vent their anger against coworkers or supervisors. Every workplace should have at least two preventive practices in place:

1. SECURITY. Always terminate an employee at the end of the day, given reasonable time to empty the desk or work area of personal belongings, and escorted by a non-threatening staff member who does any needed exit interview. It should not be possible for terminated employees to re-enter the workplace. If possible outside doors should be locked on the outside and unlocked on the inside.

A terminated employee who manages somehow to enter the building should be asked to leave, in a friendly manner, and escorted by a neutral party and not a supervisor. If an ex-employee refuses to leave the local police should be called. If the person is obviously upset and considered dangerous the call to the police should not be made in her or his presence. Your office should have an "escape route" for you and anyone upset enough to do you harm. Office furniture should be arranged so that neither you nor anyone in your office has to cross paths to leave.

2. SUPPORT. Work stress should be minimal and efforts made to humanize the work environment such as with pleasant, quiet lounge and lunch areas, earth-tone colors, comfortable furniture. If your company has a Health Department someone there should sometimes attend a staff meeting. Local mental health clinic staff may be able to make a brief presentation at a staff meeting or drop off flyers describing available services. The local mental health clinic and 24-hour crisis phone number should be prominently posted and included in the company newsletter.

SURVIVING A SHOOTOUT

The 2007 shootout at Virginia Tech was the worst campus tragedy in history. There have been shootouts in banks, restaurants, offices, and on the street. The shooters have been alone or with others, such as the pair of D.C. snipers. The reality is that a shootout can occur anywhere and at any time. Another reality is the need to prepare in advance for the possibility you may be involved in a shootout.

Try to remain calm and help others do so. If police are present, follow their directions. If you are alone or in charge, call 911 or have someone else do so. Give your location first, in case you are unable to stay on the phone. If you can't escape, hide in a locked room, lights out, shades drawn, door blocked, and lie down out of the line of fire. Call 911 again to keep police informed.

If confronted by a shooter try to remain calm. Do not raise your voice, respond angrily, or stare at the shooter. Obey all commands. Do not move in closer, reach out or touch the shooter. Do not take the weapon even if offered to you but suggest it be safely put down. Moving in forcibly is a last resort and risky as is running away, but if you do run zig-zag and used any obstacles for protective cover. Do not stop to help others. Report their location when you are at a safe distance. Keep your hands in plain view and follow police instructions. Worst case scenario: you are in the midst of people being shot. Fall down and play dead. Don't move and keep your eyes closed.

SKILL BUILDER 69. How secure and supportive is your office, department, and company? If any of the suggestions are not in place, would it be practical to implement them?

SUICIDE PREVENTION

The estimated suicide rate in the United States is 85 people a day, 30,000 every year. Another 500,000 try but don't succeed. The suicide rate is increasing. For teenagers it has quadrupled over the past 20 years and doubled for children under 14 years old. There are actually many more suicides and attempts than those reported. Many deaths in accidents are really suicides. Freud called suicide "murder in the 180th degree," self-murder, anger or rage turned around and aimed at one's self.

Why should you know anything about suicide? It happens in the workplace and in some cases is related to work. During the Great Depression, people on the street actually walked close to the curbs to avoid being struck by the bodies of men who jumped to their deaths from office windows. Suppose you happened upon a worker in your office about to jump. What would you say? What would you do? How would you feel if you were the last person who talked with someone who suicided?

You should know enough about suicide prevention to help save a life. In such an unhappy situation, it will help your mental health to realize you did all you could to prevent it. Many but not all suicidal people signal their intention beforehand. Experts estimate about a third of them do *not* give signals beforehand. Those who do don't always send clear signals. Even experienced mental health professionals can miss the clues. Here are the signal behaviors. It is rare someone will show all of them. Some who are suicidal don't openly show any.

1. Giving away prized possessions
2. Change in hygiene
3. Depressed more than usual (can seem stupid, inept, or accident-prone)
4. Personality or behavior change such as mood swings, irritability, etc.
5. Social withdrawal, especially from fun pastimes
6. Recent loss or shock
7. Increased alcohol or drug abuse

8. Increased risk taking or aggressive behavior
9. Thinks about death directly (talk, writing) or indirectly (reading, movies)
10. Has the means to do it and it's lethal
11. Previous serious attempts
12. A family member, loved one, or role model has suicided (entertainer, leader)

SUGGESTIONS

If confronted by a person who is suicidal, here are some suggestions:

1. *Consider any reference to suicide serious. Ask directly* so the point can't be missed.
2. *Be yourself.* You don't have to be a therapist or have all the answers. It's OK to be upset, even cry (shows you really care).
3. *Don't preach.* Some suicides are by impulse, a rage reaction. What you think is reassuring could backfire, especially if the person has heard many times from others.
4. *Self-disclosure* can help. If you've ever felt so depressed you wondered if it was worth living, share it. It can help a depressed person feel they're not alone and others have felt suicidal and did not act on it. It has been said that "suicide is a permanent solution to a temporary problem." Use that quote at an opportune time. Those who were saved from committing suicide almost all said later they're glad they didn't do it.
5. *Provide a safety net.* Mention others such as loved ones, clergy, local mental health clinic 24-hour phone, and AA and their AA sponsor if drinking is involved. They should know that phoning 911 gets help quickly

or they can go to any hospital ER for help. Police and hospital staffs routinely contact local mental health services where individual, group, and family therapy are available.

SKILL BUILDER 72. Do you have the phone number of your local mental health clinic or crisis line? How would you know an employee was having mental problems? Are you comfortable with the way you handle personally sensitive situations?

REALIZE SKILL 3!

Another poem by Edward Everett Hale helps realize **Skill 3:**

> I am only one, but still I am one.
> I cannot do everything, and because
> I cannot do everything
> I will not refuse to do the something I can do

FOR FURTHER STUDY

Team building

Blake, R.R., & Mouton, S. *The managerial grid.* New York: Elsevier, 1994

Katzenbach, J.R., & Smith, D.K. *Wisdom of tams: Creating the high performance organization.* New York: Harper-Collins, 2003.

Miller, B.C. *Quick team-building activities for busy managers.* New York: AMACOM, 2003.

Singer, B. *The ABC's of building a winning business.* New York: Warner Business Books, 2003.

Randolph, W.A., & Blackburn, R.S. *Managing organizational behavior.* Homewood IL: Irwin, 1989.

Yukl, G. *Leadership in organizations.* Englewood Cliffs NJ: Prentice-Hall, 2001.

Problem people

Maxwell, J.C. *Winning with people.* Nashville TN: Thomas Nelson, 2005.

Satir, V. *Peoplemaking.* Palo Alto CA: Science and Behavior Books, 1972.

Steers, R.M. *Introduction to organizational behavior.* Glenview IL: Scott Foresman, 1981.

Transformational leadership

Anderson, A., & Anderson, L A. *Beyond change management: Advanced strategies for today's transformational leaders.* New York: Wiley, 2004.

Bass, B.M. *Leadership and performance beyond expectations.* New York: Free Press, 1985.

Burns, G.M. *Leadership.* New York: Harper and Row. 1978.

Managing meetings

Balch, T.J., Evans, W.J., & Honemann, D.H. *Robert's Rules of Order in brief.* New York: DeCapo Press, 2004.

Sylvester, N. *The complete idiot's guide to Robert's Rules.* New York: Penguin Group, 2004.

SKILL 4

GET IT DONE!
You as taskmaster

Task management is *getting things done*. It includes decision-making, problem solving, and conflict management. It is the fourth and last skill because it requires a firm foundation in the three previous skills. Tasks are more easily completed when good leadership and management skills are applied. Those skills come from knowing one's self, understanding others, and coaching a close-knit team, the other three skills. In a leadership position you are called upon to be both a leader and a manager. Traditionally leadership and management were not the same. A leader's role was considered primarily *qualitative*, inspiring and motivating workers. Managers were seen in more *quantitative* terms, handling details and overseeing the completion of tasks.

Leadership does involve personality, charisma, and envisioning what can be. Management involves organizing, assigning, and monitoring, what needs to be done and how best to do it. You can be a strong leader and a weak manager, a strong manager and weak leader, or strong or weak at both. You've probably seen examples of all these variations.

For many years, leadership was defined as *influencing others to achieve goals* but there's more to it than that, and the definition is changing: "Leadership is a catalyst that transforms potential into reality, the process of influencing and supporting others to work enthusiastically toward achieving objectives"(Newstrom and Davis, 1997).

The traditional view of "getting others to do the work" is giving way to empowering workers to participate in a team approach with mentoring support. Self-actualization of leaders and followers is becoming part of leadership and management skills training. The trend is clearly to blend leadership and management skills, making leaders good managers and managers good leaders. A goal of this manual is to help you develop expertise in both areas. This fourth and final skill is to help you be more task oriented, an effective taskmaster.

SKILL BUILDER 71. *How do you rate yourself as a <u>leader</u> and as a <u>manager</u>? Equally or different? Rate each as a percentage, such as 80% leader 20% manager, etc. Big differences suggests you may need to focus more on making the two more equal.*

ENVISION THEN CREATE

Vision is an important leadership trait. Without it you are blind to opportunities to innovate and improvise. Vision flows through two stages: seeing things *as they are* and wondering *why*, and seeing (envisioning) how they *could be better* and wondering *how*. Great thinkers have been visionaries, from DaVinci and Michelangelo to the latest miracles of science and technology. This book was a vision until it was written. It was Henry Ford's vision and his assembly line that made motorcars available to thousands, Tom Edison's vision of electric power in every home, and Albert Einstein's vision of the universe that became the theory of relativity. In his mind, Columbus saw the way to the new world long before he set sail.

Shakespeare made his vision a reality, a theater and productions for everyone.

Psychiatrist Carl Jung described vision as like dreaming but while awake. It isn't the same as daydreaming though it can come at the same quiet moment of reflection. Vision emerges from a leader's ideas or the need to make changes or meet a crisis. There are Biblical references to it: "Where there is no vision people perish" (*Proverbs* 29:18). Vision is a leadership trait that separates low level achievers from great leaders. To transform a vision into reality requires both leadership and management skills. If there is only vision there will be kittle or no management. Weakness in either skill increases the risk of failure. As an effective leader you need vision to conceptualize how you can make a difference consistent with company or organization mission and core values. To have vision and follow it you need the kind of courage reflected in *John Wesley's Rule* that inspired many during the American Revolution:

> Do all the good you can,
> by all the means you can,
> in all the ways you can,
> in all the places you can,
> at all the times you can,
> to all the people you can,
> as long as ever you can (Beck, 1958).

In *Prayers of steel*, poet Carl Sandburg wrote:
> Lay me on an anvil, O God.
> Beat me and hammer me into a crowbar.
> Let me pry loose old walls.
> Let me lift and loosen old foundations (Beck, 1968).

How can your vision become real? It takes planning, organizing, staffing, directing, and monitoring. Any change should be well planned as far in advance as is possible. Potential problems should be anticipated and planned for as well. Advance information and training are important and go more smoothly when there is clear understanding and shared commitment to the change. As vision becomes reality it should be monitored to ensure continued success. When completed, celebrate with some kind of reward for all those who made it possible.

SKILL BUILDER 72. Imagine your company vanished and you were appointed to recreate it. What would you duplicate – location, layout, departments, polices, procedures? What would you replace? Why? What can be done now to improve the organization? All of this involves your vision.

LEADERSHIP POWER

Leaders are in positions of power. There are different kinds of power. Each works well in specific situations. Learning and using them will enable you to choose the one most appropriate in any situation, though more than one kind can be used at the same time. The following types of power are adapted from M. G. Aamodt's book *Applied industrial-organizational psychology*:

PERSONAL POWER: A leader's personality and charisma regardless of title or position. Works well where there is low morale. Examples: Joan of Arc, Napoleon, and Alexander the Great.

EXPERT POWER: Knowledge, skill, and experience of leaders who are known and respected for their expertise.

Works well where there is a lack information, training, or job skills. Examples: technology and sciences, Nobel Prize winners.

POSITION POWER, of an authority figure by title or relative position in the table of organization. Works well where there is change or instability. Examples: bosses, judges, police, the IRS.

REWARD POWER, recognizing or rewarding good performance. Works well when time is limited to achieve goals. Examples: mentors, teachers, coaches.

TACTICAL POWER, of "hands on" interaction and close but non-intrusive supervision. Works well where there is confusion or disorganization. Examples: military commanders and executives in crisis situations.

COERCIVE POWER, to exert pressure by reward or remand, directly or indirectly. Works well in crisis situations. Examples: Law enforcement, customs officers, wartime policies.

AFFILIATION POWER, in relating closely to others in a caring way. Works well when there is high anxiety or uncertainty. Examples: Mother Teresa, Mohandas Gandhi, Martin Luther King.

Review this list from time to time and familiarize yourself with all the kinds of power. Develop the skill use the most appropriate power type to every situation. Using an inappropriate power position increases risk of conflict.

SKILL BUILDER 73. What kinds of power are available to you? Which do you use? Are there any available to you that you don't use? As poet Robert Burns observed, it is difficult "to see ourselves as others see us," so it may be helpful to ask others which power types they see you using. What kinds of power do your superiors use? Which are not used? Why? Which could you learn to use more?

WHEN POWER IS LIMITED

It is almost impossible to have complete authority or absolute power in a job situation. Old sayings that reflect this reality:

    Man proposes; *God* disposes
    Circumstances alter all cases
    The best laid plans of mice and men often go awry

Limits to leader powers: policies and procedures, rules and regulations, structure (table of organization, levels, departmentalization, channels), and precedent (custom, tradition, corporate culture). When an organization is too informal applying leadership power can become more difficult. Directions are loosely followed, like stepping on the gas or brakes with little effect. Misinformation, poor internal communication, low morale, and the rumor mill limit efficiency and leader performance. Leader ineptness or incompetence add to these negative effects.

MANAGEMENT SKILL

Research has discovered traits of effective managers. One study (Cooper et al, 1996) found the best managers are: organizers who plan well, analyzers who are knowledgeable, and decision-makers who are steadfast and persevere to produce quality work. They delegate, are good listeners and communicators, motivate and develop others, care about people, are reassuring, supportive, and have high integrity.

SKILL BUILDER 74. Using traits of effective managers as a pass-fail checklist, how do you rate yourself? It may help to have someone else give you her/his opinion. A consensus of those asked is more likely to be more objective. Where can you improve? How will you do that?

LEAD OR FOLLOW?

There can be no leaders without followers. That's just common sense. What may not be as obvious is that effective leaders know when to lead and when to follow. *Followership* is the flip side of leadership but they are not opposites. You don't have to be out in front to lead. In many cases you should be *in* the group. You can even be in the back. Famous leaders throughout history have known there is a time when it is best to follow. Alexander the Great followed the advice of his mentor, Aristotle. Lord Nelson, England's great naval hero, often allowed officers of lesser rank to lead an attack. You can do the same by following the advice and suggestions of others and using team consensus when appropriate.

Many times a team has better judgment than you would have had making a decision alone. Many heads *can* be better than one. Delegating, appointing committees, or encouraging more discussion are other ways to use *followership* well. There are times when it is better to refer a matter to another department or person. Another way to improve this skill is consulting those in positions above or below you. If you follow more than you lead it can raise questions about your competence to make decisions and solve problems. There are times to lead directly and decisively, such as when it is necessary to interpret or apply policy and standard procedures, implement a major change and time is limited, or in an emergency situation.

SKILL BUILDER 75. How comfortable are you following others? Do you have difficulty even when another person is as able as you? When you lead are you aware of the relative competence of others who may be of help? Are you open to their help? Do you have any difficulty asking for help? What can you do to overcome any weaknesses in these areas?

Three books offer examples of the use of power. They are listed at the end of this chapter. In *Jefferson's second revolution* the 1800 Jefferson-Adams presidential campaign is described, a basic power struggle between Adams' federalists for a strong central government and Jefferson's populists who valued the rights of the individual. Those differences helped sow the seeds of the Civil War. A reality that emerged is transformational change never comes from a center moderate position but from the left or right. So, change is more possible pushing from either side rather than from the middle.

David Gergen was a White House reporter in the Carter administration and later a bipartisan adviser to presidents Nixon, Ford, Reagan, and Clinton. He had the unique vantage point of closely observing the personalities and leadership styles of five presidents. He describes seven leadership factors in his 2001 book *Eyewitness to power*. He considers the most important to be a strong quality of inner mastery. The other six factors: a central compelling purpose rooted in moral values; persuasive skill; ability to work the system; able to make a good fast start; a strong team; and passion that inspires others.

The 9/11 terrorist attack on New York occurred while Rudy Giuliani was mayor with only a few months before leaving office. His leadership was tested and his performance made him a national hero. In his 2002 book *Leadership* he described leadership as a privilege and a responsibility to get the job done. That, in turn, requires a leader's firm convictions and acceptance of accountability.

You can't really hide. No leader is *Superman* or *Wonder Woman*, so teamwork is needed that brings out the best in its members. Organizational structure and policies should match needs and focus on the mission and goals. Giuliani listed core leader skills: calm in crisis; standing up for principle; read and reflect to master a subject or skill; test truth without depending on experts; take risks judiciously and make decisions at just the right time with the right information.

WHEN TO DELEGATE

Some management consultants consider a leader's failure to delegate a sign of ineffectiveness, the leader's unwillingness or inability to share or wisely use power. This can be due to fear of losing control or a lack of confidence in workers. The leader may not see any advantage in delegating. If there is a secret to knowing when to delegate it is to "work smart, not just hard." Delegating makes everyone's job easier: the person who delegates (you!), the person delegated (empowerment), and the work unit (teamwork, morale).

There are times when it may not be wise to delegate such as when you have expertise in an area of need and time is limited. It still may be wise to ask for input from others. In most cases others will agree with you and it gives them the opportunity to be part of decision-making and work progress (participative management). Delegate too much and it may cast doubt on your decision-making ability. Some guidelines:

1. **Select the person wisely**, for their knowledge, skill, and experience.
2. **Set reasonable goals.** Goals beyond reach lower morale and motivation.
3. **Clearly explain** what's needed and your expectations. If needed, refer to relevant job orders, the position description, or policy manuals that may apply.
4. **Ensure** everyone understands, or that you've done all you can to help them do so.
5. **Monitor** progress without meddling and be available if/as needed.

SKILL BUILDER 76. *What tasks have you not delegated? Are others in the company doing more delegating than you? If so, why? Should you be delegating more? Less?*

DECISION MAKING AND PROBLEM SOLVING

It's better to solve problems when they're small. Then, they can't grow into major problems. Two approaches to problem solving and decision-making are the ***scientific method*** and ***group dynamics.***

The ***scientific method*** is used by all the sciences worldwide, evidence of its reliability and usefulness. It is an effective way to arrive at sound decisions. It's even worth memorizing so you can apply it whenever needed. There are six steps:

1. **State the problem or goal.** Unless everyone under stands the situation there can be inefficiency and wasted time. It's like a director setting the stage of a play before the actors begin. All necessary material has to be in place.
2. **Observe objectively.** It's important to see *what's there*, not what you want to see or are afraid to see. It's like being a camera that photographs what's there, no more, no less. In a sense, this step is simple since there is no need to interpret or find meaning in what is observed.
3. **Gather data.** A potential problem at this step is not gathering all the data necessary to reach a decision. Gather as much data as possible. Leave nothing out, otherwise you may overlook the most important fact or factor.
4. **Evaluate.** At this step data is studied to perceive a pattern or direction. Scientists say: "Let the data take you where it will." A potential problem at this step is relying on preconceived notions such as "that's how we've always done it" or "the boss won't like it."

    A humorous story shows the potential for error at this step. Homer and Jethro were on their first train ride. A vendor passed by selling fruit. They had never seen or eaten a banana so they bought two. They peeled it as the vendor instructed, then sat staring at it. At that moment the train went through a long tunnel and everything went black. Voice quaking, Homer asked: "Jethro, you et your'n yet?" Jethro replied: "No, I din't." "Wal, don't," Homer said nervously, "Ah took one bite and the damn thing blinded me!" Objective observation but insufficient information, evaluated poorly, reaching a wrong conclusion.

5. **Conclude.** In leadership terms this is to decide what to do then do it. Often the data points to the solution. Researchers call this "letting the data take you where it will." That's why they call the results "findings."
6. **Follow up,** the **feedback loop**. Scientists test findings by repeating (replicating) research. For you, it is the *feedback loop* of checking back, testing a decision, and making any changes. It is the most important step. Without a feedback loop a decision runs by itself like a runaway train. Quality assurance is a way to monitor how well decisions are working.

SKILL BUILDER 77. How can you apply the scientific method to your decision-making? Do you use feedback loops? Management consultants consider feedback loops essential and a high priority need.

Are there situations when using the scientific method is unwise? Not really, but there is a joke about being scientifically objective and factually correct with tragic results. During the French Revolution a physician, a priest, and a scientist were to be executed by the guillotine. The executioner asked the physician if he wanted to be executed face up or face down. He chose to be face down and was put in that position. The guillotine was triggered. The blade jammed half way down. According to French law you went free if an execution failed. The priest was next and asked to be face up. Again the guillotine was triggered but jammed. The priest went free. The scientist asked to be face up. But, just before the guillotine was triggered, he said: "Oh, I see the problem. There's a knot in the rope up there." So, you can be 100% right – and dead wrong!

SKILL BUILDER 78. Hopefully you will never be in a situation where fact finding would have negative results, as the engineer in the guillotine. However, if your are ever in a situation where no one wanted to hear the facts and you were the only one with objective data, would you be able to hold your ground and "tell it like it is?"

USE GROUP DYNAMICS

The scientific method is an effective way to solve a problem or reach a decision but it is mainly an individual method. Using group dynamics shares decision making with others. The group process begins with the leader's effort to recognize and constructively use worker input. Involving a group enables everyone in the group to participate and experience the satisfaction of completing a task. It is "people power," an exchange of gifts that builds teamwork and increases morale. It mutual need satisfaction where participants share their knowledge, experience, and skills. This enhances fellow and family feeling beyond the boss-employee relationship.

SKILL BUILDER 79. Using the group process involves a delicate balance between thinking and feeling. A 50-50 thinking-feeling balance might seem reasonable and logical but many effective leaders rely mainly on thinking and less on feeling. Some leaders show little or no feelings interacting with workers. For people to say "I'd follow (her or him) through the gates of hell" they must have positive feelings for that leader. That doesn't happen unless the leader's feelings toward them are positive and obvious. What's your thinking and feeling percentiles?

It's as inefficient to think too much as it is to feel too much, to overdo or underdo.

MANAGING CHANGE

Leadership is easy when everything goes well but that 6s rarely so. Managing change is an "acid test" of leader competence. Change can be sudden and dramatic, a surprise or shock to everyone, or gradual. Either way it usually means some painful readjustment. Today, change often comes in the form of downsizing, streamlining, computerization, or changing technology. When there is sudden change, very little if anything done in the past is of much help.

To effectively manage change it is wise to closely monitor how workers adapt to it. Reassure them and continue to maintain optimal speed to complete the change. It's a balancing act between maintaining morale and motivation and making the change. Some guidelines:

1. **Inform**. Initially report the facts without exaggeration or bias, and repeat as needed.
2. **Improvise.** Innovate ways to keep everyone on target and vent frustration.
3. **Train** for change. Anticipate. Overlearning helps smoothe the process.
4. **Implement** the change. Tolerate early errors. Maintain 2-way communications and "family feeling."
5. **Do it!** Then, over time ensure the change becomes routine, the new standard.

A positive aspect of change is the opportunity for personal and professional growth, for you and everyone else. Some ideas you can share to help effect change and personal and professional growth:

1. **Learning is change and change is lifelong.** When Socrates was asked to define intelligence he replied: "Intelligence is to know what you don't know." You can help workers adjust to change pointing out it is no longer possible to know something and never need to learn any more about it. Examples are the changing technology in aircraft, cars, TVs, computers, and appliances. The list is endless. What we know today is further improved (changed) tomorrow. Isaac Newton said: "There is nothing constant in nature but change."

2. **We can do it. Others have.** Build on individual and team strengths and pride. This develops a "can do" attitude. The motto of army engineers in World War 2 was: "The difficult we do immediately. The impossible takes a little longer." Change can be a challenge and opportunity for the team and every team member to "show what they got!"

3. **Make it personal,** an opportunity for you and those you lead to use the change as a springboard to self-actualization. The most beautiful flower grows from a tiny seed through dark soil, forms a strong stem to rise up into the sun then blossom. It isn't easy but what a beautiful end product!

4. **Celebrate every step forward.** Use even the tiniest step to recognize and reward work well done, individually and the team or department. As old LaoTse wrote: "The journey of 1000 miles begins with the first step; a 9-storied terrace begins with the first clump of dirt."

SKILL BUILDER 80. *Do you use any of these techniques to help manage change? Think of a change in your own or another department or company. Were any of these methods used? If not, would they have helped? Reflect on how you might use them.*

CONFLICT MANAGEMENT
THE TALE OF TWO CAPTAINS

Two British naval officers were ship's captains at the time "Britannia ruled the waves." Both faced serious conflicts and are examples of the right way and wrong way to manage conflict. William Bligh was sailing master on Cook's *HMS Resolution* before he took command of *HMS Bounty.* His log when rounding Cape Horn reported seas so rough the yardarm touched wave crests. It took ten months to reach Tahiti where *Bounty* was anchored for five months. Three of the ship's crew deserted, were found and given 48 lashes.

Fletcher Christian was 24 when he led the mutiny that set Bligh adrift in a longboat with 18 others. Bligh sailed 3618 miles to Timor without a chart, an amazing feat even today. He was appointed Governor of New South Wales, Australia. His staff put him under house arrest then sent him to England in chains. Acquitted despite his poor record of conflict management he was promoted to Rear Admiral and retired as a Vice Admiral.

As Bligh circled the world with Captain Cook, Horatio Nelson was aboard a ship exploring the Arctic. He was later posted to the West and East Indies in command of a frigate. Nelson helped lay siege to Toulon and in the invasion of Corsica where he lost sight in his right eye. He led the victory over the Spanish fleet off Portugal and the amphibious assault on the Canary Islands where his badly wounded right arm had to be amputated.

Nelson's victory over the French fleet at the Battle of the Nile prevented Napoleon's invasion of Egypt. His most famous achievement was defeating the combined French and Spanish fleets at Trafalgar where he was mortally wounded. Nelson rose from Captain to Vice Admiral, then to Viscount and Fleet Commander. Bligh's rigid inflexibility led to dissension and mutiny. Nelson empowered his officers, allowing them to help plan strategy and lead attacks. He related to sailors with humor and fellow feeling. Both captains did their duty as they saw it. Both were promoted. Bligh leaves behind only a gravestone and is remembered as the cause of a historic mutiny. Nelson's statue stands high on a column in London's Trafalgar Square and is remembered as one of the world's greatest naval heroes.

CONFLICT: GOOD AND BAD

Conflict is a negative word for many people, triggering memories of bad times, frustrating situations or "mental unfinished business." Few people remember them as positive experiences. But, the reality is:

Conflict is inevitable. As time passes, differences emerge that cause conflict between people, organizations and employees, and employees and supervisors.

Unresolved conflict is destructive. It can cause hurt feelings, festering anger and resentment, low morale, poor teamwork, high turnover, and becomes "mental unfinished business" that persists and stagnates.

Conflict can be transformed negative to positive and is an acid test of effective leadership. Every conflict is a challenge and opportunity to find new and different ways to cope with and resolve it by clearer communication, better understanding, and closer teamwork. It is possible to disagree without being disagreeable and to generate light from heat. Benefits are improved morale, personal and professional growth and self-actualization for everyone.

Conflict is good when it *stimulates* new ideas and constructive criticism, *challenges* outmoded policies and procedures so they can be updated, *uncovers alternatives* and *improvements, increases participation,* all of which *strengthens and unifies* the team toward resolution, *raising morale.* Conflict is *not* good when it *wastes time* (takes longer to get things done), *raises stress levels* (unvented stress accumulates), *drains energy* (unresolved conflict is exhausting), *fosters apathy* (erodes enthusiasm and initiative), and *nothing is done about it* (negatives increase, positives fade), all of which *lowers morale.*

SKILL BUILDER 81. How much of Nelson and how much of Bligh are in your leadership style in conflict situations? Are you satisfied with that balance? How can you improve it?

CONFLICT BETWEEN GROUPS

While friendly competition between teams or departments is healthy and boosts morale it can lead to conflict situations with negative impact. Research has isolated these typical areas most frequently involved:

1. **Interdependence.** Conflict can occur when a team or department depends on one person's expertise or the work

of a others outside the team or department. *Pooled interdependence* is when there is sharing and interaction of everyone involved. It prevents conflict. *Sequential interdependence* is when shared work progresses in steps such as purchasing raw materials to production to warehousing and inventory to promotion and sales. Negative potential in both types is unreliability, inefficiency, or incompetence of anyone in the flow of work.

2. Differentiation, based on *different* functions of teams or departments. Goals and objectives may differ just enough to cause conflict. Accounting, design, and production seek the best product at least cost, but promotion and sales want higher quality and distinctive features to compete in the marketplace. The enthusiasm of a work unit to achieve its goals can cause unhealthy competition and conflict within the organization. If a work unit becomes dominant it can have a demoralizing effect on others.

3. Limited resources. When needed resources are limited or not available, even for good reason, there can be a win-lose battle for them. Examples are lack of funds, shortages of materials, limited staff or training, and delayed paperwork flow. Adverse effects can be reduced by leaders who inspire and motivate, worker loyalty to the company, team, or department, close teamwork, and brainstorming for more innovative ways to meet goals.

4. Reward and recognition help increase self-esteem and self-actualization. This psychic income can be paid by as little as a smile, an approving nod, or a verbal "pat on the back" in memos of appreciation and newsletter items that reward and recognize worker achievement, service, or special skills. These motivate, raise morale, and ensure optimal production and product quality. Reward and recognition cost nothing and it is surprising how little is done in this area.

5. Communications. *Poor communication* is a frequent complaint of employees at all levels. Unclear or too little communication leads to confusion, frustration, error, and disillusionment. Hurried or incomplete information, lack of follow up, excessive jargon and technical terms are examples of poor communications, negative factors that can separate and antagonize departments and work units and lead to conflict and heated confrontation.

SKILL BUILDER 82. Apply each conflict risk factor to your firm and department. Where are they strong? What can you do to overcome any weaknesses?

COPING SKILLS

STRATEGIES

Two leadership strategies to cope with conflict are by being *assertive* or *cooperative* (Thomas, 1977) and can be charted on a graph to show their relative effectiveness. Degrees of *assertiveness* are on the vertical axis and *cooperativeness* is on the horizontal. Conflicts handled in the lower left section are *lose-lose*, those in the upper left and lower right are *win-lose*, and those in the upper right are *win-win*.

```
A
S    compete                    collaborate
S
E
R           compromise
T
I
V    avoid                      accommodate
E
            COOPERATIVE
```

SKILL BUILDER 83. Where would you place your conflict strategy on the graph? How assertive and cooperative are you? What percentile of each? Are you satisfied with that combination? If not, what can you do to make your conflict strategy more effective?

MANAGEMENT STYLE

McClelland and Burnham (1976) described leader-worker interaction as a comparison of two management styles: *affiliation* and *power*. They used a 10-point scale to compare affiliation and power as opposing forces. They called power "the great motivator" for leaders, based on goals, objectives, and tasks to achieve them, and affiliation as a focus mainly on people and relationships. Their graphic formulation:

```
Laissez-faire       Team leader         Taskmaster
(anything goes)                       (rigid authority)
    1    2    3    4    5    6    7    8    9    10
```

Conflict resolution strategies fall on a line between these two force fields. The middle or moderate position is most flexible, enabling the leader to maintain contact wit both extremes and anyone in the middle where most workers are. The *team leader* is a middle ground position that allows the most flexibility to resolve conflict. Of course, there are situations where a laissez-faire or taskmaster approach is more appropriate.

SKILL BUILDER 84. Where on the management style scale do you place yourself? Is it where you would like to be? If not, what can you do to function there?

INFLUENCE TACTICS

Influence tactics are how power is applied. Yukl (1981) described nine ways power influences others:

Persuade with information, logically and rationally.
Legitimize, by referring to policies, procedures, manuals, or precedents.
Consult with a sampling of authorities, workers, or others.
Peer or group pressure using group consensus or from other groups to pressure the undecided.
Personal pressure by frequently checking back, reminding, and questioning.
Personal appeal, seeking work or support as a personal favor.
Fellow or family feeling by recognition, reward, or special treatment.
Inspiration, appealing to principle, ideals, or values.
Make a deal by mutual exchange of work, materials, or favors.

SKILL BUILDER 85. On a blank sheet make three columns: OFTEN USE, USE SOMETIMES, and NEVER USE. Rate your use of the nine influence tactics by sorting them in the three columns. The result is your influence style. Satisfied with it? If not, what can you do to improve?

CONFLICT ANALYSIS

Conflict analysis is also called *locus of control,* and is similar to the *monkey on your back* concept you may have heard of. Often a worker starts a conversation with: "we have a problem." It's the first move on the conflict analysis chessboard. If you don't counter it, the conflict situation becomes *your* problem, a monkey on your back. Conflict analysis is a 3-step system of assessing then processing conflict:

1. Anticipate and analyze *who owns the problem.*
   There are three possibilities:
   (a) you
   (b) someone else
   (c) something else (work unit, department, company).

2. *The owner of the problem should solve it!* If it's you, take appropriate action. If it's someone else, that person should solve it. If it's something else, that something should solve it.

3. Be aware of *positive and negative influences* on you, others, and the work unit as the problem is processed and solved. That will vary with time, the situation, and the problem solver. Monitor closely to encourage and

support problem solving. It is far better to wait a bit then reward and recognize the problem solver than to crowd, hurry, or show impatience. Of course, there are situations when you have to take charge to avoid costly mistakes. Even then, explain why you do so. That helps others learn and grow personally and professionally.

SECRET: *Don't solve problems. See that they get solved!*

SKILL BUILDER 86. An employee on your staff makes abrasive comments at meetings and in interactions with others. One worker resigned in disgust. Who owns the problem? How would you get it solved?

RESOLUTION STRATEGY

Even though they seem to be opposing factors, there is really "wiggle room," a space for maneuvering between *competition* and *cooperation.* Newstrom and Davis (1997) listed tactics for functioning in that space:

Soothe and smooth by complimenting the other side and sharing similarities and areas of agreement.

Negotiate, compromise to find a middle ground, a fair and shared solution or to explore alternatives.

Persuade by stating your position with facts and reasons and suggesting solutions.

Confront frankly so the other side knows where you will not yield or change your position.

Refer out to committees from both sides or a 3rd person (expert, consultant, or mediator) to explore common ground and possible solutions.

Fight by trying to impose only your position and not yielding on key points.

Flight, avoiding, or withdrawing by tabling it to some

other time to meet again when you've regrouped with more data or to close the door permanently to future discussion.

Flight is considered *lose-lose*, smoothing as *lose-win*, forcing as *win-lose*, compromise as *indecisive* if there is no clear outcome, and confrontation as *win-win*. They recommend confrontation because positions are clear and open with little of value negotiated away. To confront effectively you must fully understand the issue, strengths and weaknesses of both sides, the alternatives and costs. There are many variables and situations where any of the seven positions may be as effective. It isn't always simple, so be versatile, flexible, and able to function in whatever mode is appropriate at the time and situation.

SKILL BUILDER 87. Which strategy are you most comfortable using? Which are difficult for you? Why? Try to be able to use whichever is most appropriate.

MINIMIZE CONFLICT STRESS

While it may not be possible to eliminate or avoid conflict you can lessen its potential negative effect on you and prevent it from getting worse. Here's how:

FIND YOUR SHANGRI-LA

Guided imagery is a self-relaxation technique used by mental health professionals to neutralize the negative effect of stress. To use it visualize a relaxing imaginary place, somewhere you can always go to escape from stress. Many people choose a sandy ocean beach, others a beautiful garden or forest. Avoid imagining a real place.

That can bring on memories and other "busy" thoughts that can interfere. You must be alone. If others are there it is a shared social interaction no longer personal. If you find strolling along a beach relaxing imagine it *in slow motion*. Jogging or purposeful walking are not conducive to deeper relaxation.

During the day, imagine your peaceful place whenever you can take a break, such as sitting for a quiet moment after breakfast, at your desk at work, while waiting for someone, in a comfortable chair or sofa at home, even sitting on the toilet. Take a deep breath and go there several times a day to strengthen the relaxing effect and imaginary visualization. In time it becomes automatic. You will take a deep breath without thinking about it and imagine your peaceful place whenever you begin to feel stressed. You'll know it's working as your body relaxes.

For maximum effect, once a day lie down in a restful position, preferably on your back, legs slightly apart, head on a pillow or in a recliner chair. A 30-minute cassette recorder that clicks off at tape end can provide 15 minutes on one side. Some find it helpful to play soft music at low volume for the 15 minutes. Others record the ocean surf sound of TV static from a blank channel. It's similar to white sound widely used in relaxation therapy. Some just use a blank tape that clicks off at 15 minutes just to mark the end of the time period. Use whatever works best for you.

To further strengthen the relaxing effect picture yourself in your peaceful place every night as you fall asleep. In a comfortable position, eyes closed, take one or two long, slow deep breaths, fall asleep in your peaceful place switching back to normal breathing. If you awaken during the night, return to sleep by visualizing your peaceful place. Be there.

To deepen the effect, focus on details such as sand, grass, flowers, trees, birds, the sky (with or without clouds), a soft breeze, the scent of flowers or pine needles, etc. If you have a busy mind and everyday thoughts creep in, *don't fight them*. That uses energy and isn't relaxing. Instead, consider them like a TV commercial of no interest. You see them but don't attend to them. Invading thoughts will fade as you focus on details in your peaceful place and as you gain more experience going there.

Using guided imagery day and night shapes it into a powerful mental defense. When rushed or in a conflict situation you can take a deep breath and envision your peaceful place. It should not be a breath like a sigh but just a little deeper than usual so no one will notice. An obvious sigh can send a negative message to others that you're bored or impatient.

Use a relaxing posture to help you find and keep a stable, balanced state of mind. When sitting place both feet on the floor and sit erect, balancing and centering yourself. If standing, put weight equally on both feet. Walk just a bit slower except as exercise when a faster pace is better.

When stressed, be aware of your breathing. Keep it regular, not hurried. Anxiety often causes faster breathing and can lead to hyperventilation. It is almost impossible to become upset if your breathing rate is normal and your body is stable and balanced. Annoying interruptions can be deactivated by pairing them with the relaxing details in your peaceful place. If you have a bad day take a short break and, alone in a quiet place, sit down, close your eyes, take a deep breath, and for a few minutes relax in your peaceful place. Guided imagery is an instant stress reliever, a non-drug tranquilizer.

SKILL BUILDER 88. What's your peaceful place? Focus on its details. Find quiet places at work and at home where you can practice and strengthen guided imagery.

DEVELOP AN EARLY WARNING SYSTEM

Another way to minimize the negative effect of stress is to develop your own *early warning system* at the first sign of stress. What happens to you when you are stressed? What is the first sign? Everyone has a weak spot where anxiety is first felt. For some it's a dry mouth, for others it's a change in voice tone, throbbing in the head, rapid heart rate, fast or shallow breathing, butterflies in the stomach, or a nervous twitch.

Being instantly aware of your body's first sign of stress *is* your early warning system. As soon as you feel it, imagine your peaceful place, take a break, switch and do something else, or change your routine. Doing nothing allows stress to build.

SKILL BUILDER 89. What is your body's first sign of stress? Experiment with matching it with the image of your peaceful place and its details. Develop this skill so that it turns on automatically whenever needed.

WHEN CONFLICT IS 1-TO-1

Despite your best efforts you may find yourself face-to-face with someone in a heated and difficult situation. Some suggestions:

1. *Ensure uninterrupted privacy* to prevents others being demoralized or upset.
2. *Keep focused.* Avoid distractions and tangents. Use small talk to establish rapport and personalize the conversation but keep it minimal.
3. *Use I-WE statements* not I-you that can inflame the situation.
4. *Be cool, stay calm.* Don't get emotional. Stick to facts. Keep it positive.
5. **Switch to** *scientific problem solving.* You can't go wrong doing so.
6. *Explore alternatives,* pro and con, theirs and yours, but don't get lost in them.
7. *"Bird dog."* Follow up with a feedback loop to ensure standards are met.

SKILL BUILDER 90. On a separate sheet make three columns: ALWAYS USE, USE SOMETIMES, and DON'T USE. Sort the suggested coping strategy and tactics under one of the headings. This shows your coping style. Try them all to be more versatile.

WHEN YOU ARE THE PROBLEM

There are situations where *you* are the major problem:

Getting fired! "Fired" is an interesting word for being terminated from a job (another fascinating term for it). *Fired* can bring up negative images of pain, the flames of hell, or one of the worst days of your life. But there are positive images as well such as the test of fire. Metals are fired to form stronger alloys and to temper (strengthen) steel. Being fired is a disappointment or shock if there is no forewarning. It may seem ironic but it could also be the best thing that can happen to you. It is an opportunity for you to learn more about yourself. A theme throughout this manual is finding something positive in any negative experience. Every failure is a lesson for future success. Getting fired can be a wake up call, a reality check of what you've done and could have done, how and why you can do better on the next job. It can be the key to unlock your real potential.

Being fired provides you with hard data to check out yourself, the company, and the factors that caused the termination. You may have been in the wrong job with the wrong company, perhaps even in the wrong field. Use insight into these factors to grow personally and professionally. Higher management may have erred in hiring you (their mistake). The position may not have matched your ability and experience (your mistake). It may be that stress burned you out. It may have been bad luck (business downturn). Be open to the factors that caused you're being fired, despite the hurt. Any termination means change, not just changing jobs, but an opportunity to change your mind about your career. Between jobs you can reflect on finding "a better fit" in another organization with a fresh new start.

Being fired can jolt you to explore positions at other levels or other kinds of business or services. Many who are fired discover they've been in the wrong business or in the wrong position. Right now, hopefully long before your present position is in danger, you can prepare yourself for any possibility of failure by:

1. *Keep your resume updated.* Word it positively. Keep it brief (1 or 2 pages). Puff it up but don't lie (too risky).

2. *Maintain a "brag file"* of references, testimonial letters, and performance evaluations. Do this whenever you change jobs or get promoted. Without it you may not be able to locate source persons who have moved or died and are no longer available.
3. *Keep your finger on the pulse of the field,* who's hiring, at what levels and salaries. Read the help wanted ads and keep your resume on file with recruiters ("head hunters"). Some executives apply and interview for jobs even though they decline offers. One commented: "It keeps me fresh and there's always the chance the job of a lifetime will be among them."
4. *Regularly ask your boss for feedback* and areas for Improvement. Don't overdo it, but do it. If you're doing well the feedback will boost your self-esteem. It might even jog management toward a raise or even a promotion. If you're not doing well it will be an early warning to exert more effort, make changes, or think about a transfer or graceful exit where you can do better.
5. *Fire yourself!* Some executives have *fired themselves*, realizing they were the wrong person in the wrong place at the wrong time and those factors were not likely to change from negative to positive. *They* were the only factor that could change. If you are in that frame of mind, it may help to check with trusted friends or a management recruiter. You may be hypersensitive and over-reacting.

SKILL BUILDER 91. Is your resume updated? Are you on file with a management recruiter? Are you maintaining a brag file? If you were fired today would you look for a similar position in the same field? What other fields and at what other levels could you work well?

EVALUATING PEOPLE

Most companies and government agencies have a formal system of performance evaluation. The rationale is to set and maintain standards and to ensure optimal productivity. It provides documentation of strengths and weaknesses to identify high and low achievers. While maintaining standards is a management function, motivating workers is a leadership skill. For workers, meeting and surpassing standards and goals boost self-esteem and satisfy self-actualization needs. When they are done well, performance evaluations give workers useful feedback, and recognizes achievement as well as identifying areas for improvement and goals for the next evaluation cycle. Informal chats are a less painful way to let workers "know where they stand" and lessen the "doom's day" anxiety many workers have about formal evaluation sessions.

A frequent evaluation error is having only one performance interview a year. Evaluation should be an ongoing process, not an annual event. Workers should have a realistic idea of the quality of their work at any time. That makes formal, scheduled face-to-face evaluations less stressful. Annual reviews mean a whole year passes before workers are informed about their performance. Today's workplace is subject to many changes within a year and more frequent evaluations are more effective. Then, employees with deficiencies have more opportunity to improve their work and with more frequent feedback.

Another problem is *inconsistent scoring.* There are "hard markers" and "easy markers." Supervisors should be in substantial agreement as to what is good, fair, or unacceptable work quality. The worst case scenario is when unsatisfactory work is passed, minimized, or ignored. Ironically, it's usually not the easy marker most at fault, but the on-line direct super-visor who observe workers daily and firsthand.

While performance rating systems vary from one firm or agency to another there are similar problem areas:

1. *Central tendency error* is when leaders rate tasks as completed not *how well* they were done.
2. *Strict or lenient error* is by a rater who is overly strict or overly lenient. Either extreme does not help workers realize their strengths and weaknesses.
3. *Halo effect* is the tendency to rate all tasks or skills equally, such as rating everything good or above average even when it isn't, as if the worker has a halo overhead that everything is above average. *Horns* might be an appropriate term for low ratings in everything, usually because there's a major deficiency in one or more performance factors.
4. *Recency error* is a rating based on recent work rather than throughout the entire evaluation period.
5. *Personal bias* is when an evaluator rates a worker knowingly or unknowingly based more on personal opinion than an objective evaluation of work done. This is a high risk where there are gender, racial, ethnic, or age differences. A variation is *similar-to-me bias* when a workers score inappropriately high because of they have a similar background to the rater.

6. *First impression error* is when an initial impression is carried over into an evaluation rather than actual performance throughout the evaluation period.
7. *Unclear language.* "Average" or "good" can have different meanings to different raters. Evaluation forms and performance criteria should be worded clearly. Raters should be trained in the performance standards. What is said to workers can be interpreted differently by them. Constructive criticism cushioned too softly may have little or no impact and the worker could respond when confronted later with: "I didn't think it was that much of a problem" or "it wasn't made clear to during the evaluation." A way to ensure there is mutual understanding is to ask workers to reflect back what they were told about areas for improvement. This also prevents hypersensitive workers exaggerating their weaknesses.

SKILL BUILDER 92. *What is your opinion of performance appraisal systems you've been subjected to and have used to evaluate others? Were the forms clearly worded? Did they realistically describe the scope of work and the proficient standard (pass-fail, good-fair-poor, numerical rating)? How can the system you're using be improved?*

EVALUATING PROGRAMS

If there was no need to evaluate programs we'd still be riding horses to work! Millions are spent on program evaluations by teams of experts. It involves meticulous attention to every detail of a company's operations. You need a Zen "3rd eye" to see things others miss. Working in a company or agency can make it difficult to see how operations compare with other companies or agencies. It's difficult to see the forest when all you see are the trees in front of you. The key to effective program evaluation is to see your department or company with that Zen third eye, as if by a disinterested observer or unbiased spectator. Program evaluation should be ongoing and not a special event. Here are some ways to do it:

1. *Sacred cow* (Kriegel and Brandt, 1996). This is really a variation of *brainstorming,* by scrutinizing a standard, policy or procedure in a free and open discussion where it is understood there are no dumb questions. Tedious detailed nitpicking or tangents are acceptable.
2. *Checklists* when done well ensure that important factors will be checked and notations made if needed. It is better than relying on a verbal or written report that may omit or minimize something important. Airline pilots and NASA astronauts use checklists to ensure safety and proficiency. Why don't you?
3. *Experts and consultants* with knowledge and experience in a subject or similar operation bring with them a fresh new look with little or no personal bias or evaluation errors. They can be managers in other agencies or firms, academics, or experienced retirees.
4. *Read-study-compare.* Studying books on the subject, surfing the Internet, and visiting other companies with similar programs are low-cost ways to get useful evaluation information.

SKILL BUILDER 93. *A manager of another department or in another firm asks you to visit for a day and do a program evaluation. Assuming the firm is not competitive and there are no other obstacles in the way, how would* you do it? Take time and make notes. It can help you see ways to evaluate your own operation.

SKILL BUILDER 94. This is the final exercise, intended to bring closure to the four skills.
1. If the skill builders in this book were an examination for a leadership position, how would you scored on it? Are you satisfied with that performance?
2. What have you learned from this manual that you can use immediately? Make a contract with yourself to do it. Promise yourself or your group you will.
3. Find a trusted contract partner to give you feedback on your progress and suggestions for improvement. Do the same for your contract partner.

REALIZE SKILL 4!

It's graduation time! There are two parting thoughts to help you realize the **Skill 4.** Remember, developing leadership skills is an ongoing process. Keep this book handy. Refer back to it regularly to keep you up to speed in your personal and professional growth. The parting thoughts reflect the wisdom of West and East. The first is attributed to St. Francis of Assisi:

> *God, grant me the serenity*
> *to accept what cannot be changed,*
> *the courage to change what should*
> *be changed, and the wisdom*
> *to know the difference*

The second is from Gautama Siddhartha, the Buddha, 2500 years ago:

*As the elephant endures the arrow
so, you should patiently bear abuse
-- there are many unkind archers!*

FOR FURTHER STUDY
Decision making, problem solving
Vroom, V.H., & Yetton, P. *Leadership and decision making.* Pittsburgh PA: University of Pittsburgh Press., 1973
Managing change
Bridges, W. *Managing transitions: Making the most of change.* New York: Perseus, 2003.
Conflict management
Thomas, K. Conflict and conflict management. In M.D. Dunnette (Ed.), *Handbook of industrial and organizational psychology.* Chicago IL: Rand McNally, 1977.
Peters, T. *Thriving on chaos.* New York: Knopf, 1987.
Walton, R.E. *Managing conflict: Interpersonal dialogue and third party roles.* Reading MA: Addison-Wesley, 1987.
Evaluating people and programs
Bass, B.M. *Leadership and performance beyond expectations.* New York: Free Press, 1985.
Cooper, M., Kaufman, G., & Hughes, W. Measuring supervisory potential. *IPMA News*, December 1996.
Herzberg, F. *Work and the nature of man.* Cleveland OH: World, 1966.
Leadership-management theory
Aamodt, M.G. *Applied industrial-organizational psychology.* Pacific Grove CA: Brooks/Cole, latest edition.
Murchinsky, P.M. *Psychology applied to work.* Pacific Grove CA: Brooks/Cole, latest edition.
Newstrom, J.W., & Davis, K. *Organizational behavior: Human behavior at work.* New York: McGraw-Hill, 1997.

Power and influence

Cohen, A.R., & Bradford, D. L. *Influence without authority.* New York: Wiley, 1990.

Dunn, S. *Jefferson's second revolution.* New York: Houghton-Mifflin, 2004.

Eddy, W.B., & Burke, W.W. *Behavioral science and the manager's role.* San Diego CA: University Associates, 1980.

Gergen, D. *Eyewitness to power: The essence of leadership, Nixon to Clinton.* New York: Simon and Schuster, 2001.

Giuliani, R., & Kuson, K. *Leadership.* New York: Miramax Books, 2002.

Hunt, J.G., & Larson, L.L. (Eds.) *Leadership: The cutting edge.* Carbondale IL: Southern Illinois University, 1977.

Kriegel, R., & Brandt, D. *Sacred cows make the best burgers.* New York: Warner, 1996.

McClelland, D.C., & Burnham, D.H. Power is the great motivator. *Harvard Business Review,* 54(2), 102-104. Cambridge MA: Harvard University Press, 1976.

O'Hanlon, W. *Taproots.* New York: Norton, 1987.

Yukl, G. *Leadership in organizations.* Englewood Cliffs NJ: Prentice-Hall.

INDEX

Agendas, meeting, 108
Assert-cooperate grid, 148
Behaviorism, 31
Body language, 59
Burnout, fight it, 42
Chairing meetings, 104
Change managing, 142
Conflict: analysis, 151; among groups, 146; managing, 144; when it is 1-to-1, 157
Congruence, 58
Counseling skills, 86
Decisionmaking, 138
Defenses, verbal, 62
Delegate, when, how, 137
Discrimination, 120
Dissatisfier-satisfier, 103
Diversity, 113, 115
Empathy, 116
Ethnicity, 15
Evaluating: people, 160; programs, 162
Five-factor theory, 35
Followership, 135
Forces that shape you, 13
Freud's theory, 32
Friends, 17
Games, verbal, 68
Genetic traits, 13
Group: dynamics, 141; identity, 16; power, 91
Harassment, 120
Hidden agendas, 73
Home and family, 16
Humanistic psychology, 33
Influence tactics, 150

Interacting-transacting, 64
Intimacy, sharing, 72
Isms, 24, 120
Johari window, 57
KISS simplicity, 36
Listening skill, ABC, 55
Locus of control, 151
Management style, 149
Managerial grid, 98
Memory, improving, 41.
Mentoring, 85
Miniscript, 45
Needs, 25; unmet, 26; sick, 27
Negatives, neutralizing, 111
Obstacles to perception, 20
Occupation, effect of, 19
Parliamentary procedure, 109
Personality, 30
Positive, choose to be, 122
Power: leader, 132; limits of, 134
Problem people, 73
Problem solving, 138
Psychodynamic theory, 32
Resolution strategy, 152
School, effect of, 18
Self-actualization, 26, 29
Scientific method, 138
Social status, 18
Speak up, 38
Stress, minimizing, 153
Suicide prevention, 125
Talk tactics, 83
Team: ideal leader, 101; ideal member, 94; team or group, 90

Think on your feet, 37
Time and timing, 104
Traits and types, 34
Transactional analysis, 64
Transformational leadership, 99
Unique, you are, 12
Use the group, 82, 141
Verbal defenses, 62
Violence, workplace, 123
Vision, 100, 119, 130
V's, the three, 119
Write right, 40
Zen leadership, 47

OTHER BOOKS by Frank MacHovec

Light from the East: A gathering of Asian wisdom. Berkeley, CA: Stone Bridge Press.

… and these from www.lulu.com …

Exploring inner space: The voyage of self-doscovery

Divine spark: Spiritual intelligence in you and the universe

Buddha, Tao, Zen" Mystic triad

Pocket I Ching

Pocket Tao

Pocket Buddha

www.ingramcontent.com/pod-product-compliance
Lightning Source LLC
Chambersburg PA
CBHW051758040426
42446CB00007B/432